Men Who Conquered

Men Who Conquered

By

JOHN T. FARIS

ESSAY INDEX

Essay Index Reprint Series

BOOKS FOR LIBRARIES PRESS

FREEPORT, NEW YORK

First Published 1922
Reprinted 1968

LIBRARY OF CONGRESS CATALOG CARD NUMBER:

68-55846

MANUFACTURED
BY
HALLMARK LITHOGRAPHERS, INC.
IN THE U.S.A.

Foreword

IT is not necessary that the subject of a biography should be a famous man in order that his story may be interesting and helpful. Doctor Johnson said that there is not a man in the street whose biography ought not to be made interesting, provided he could narrate something of his experiences of life, his trials, his difficulties, his successes and his failures.

Of the fifteen men whose life stories are sketched in *Men Who Conquered,* some became famous, while some lived and died in obscurity. But all of them achieved splendid things, in the face of difficulties and discouragements almost without number. So it is well that others who long to surmount obstacles shall look to them for inspiration and courage.

J. T. F.

Philadelphia, Pa.

Contents

7

Contents

I

The Evolution of a Merchant Prince

How William E. Dodge Achieved His Ambition

ONE day in 1820, in the general country store
at Bozrahville, Connecticut, the proprietor
called aside his fourteen-year-old son, who
had been his assistant for some time, and said:

" It pleases me to see you making such headway.
I have set apart this showcase at this end of the
store for your very own. Stock it to suit yourself.
Whatever you make here shall be yours alone."

This was the real beginning of the career of
the famous merchant-philanthropist, William E.
Dodge, who was born in Hartford, Connecticut,
September 4, 1805. He had attended school till he
was twelve years old, then had served as clerk in a
New York store in which his father had an interest,
and, in 1819, had been transferred to the store connected with the cotton mill owned by his father.

When the counter was given him for his very
own, William watched eagerly for the coming of
the next peddler, and from him he bought his first
stock of novelties with which he hoped to tempt the
pennies and nickels and dimes from the pockets of
juvenile visitors to the store. Older people, too,

paused to see the tempting display, attracted more, perhaps, by the courteous bearing of the popular clerk than by the goods he sold. There were many customers who were unwilling to be served by any one else; and when they learned that the counter was a venture of his own they were glad to encourage him by their purchases.

Close application to business and the frequent substitution of crackers and cheese for more substantial meals brought on serious illness. When the young clerk was able to leave the sick room, the physician prescribed plenty of life in the open air; so he arranged to turn peddler for a season. In a wagon without springs he carried his small stock in trade from house to house along the Connecticut roads, increased the circle of his acquaintance as well as his savings, and, what was of still more consequence, added to the experience without which capital would have been of small benefit to him. When he was able to return to the store, his father had such confidence in his ability that he sent him to New York to buy goods for the entire establishment. The boy showed good judgment on this occasion, and he was sent again on a similar errand. It was soon an understood thing that he was the purchasing agent for the store. In those days a trip to New York, whether made by stage coach or by sailing vessel, was a serious undertaking.

Fortunately for the aspiring young business man, his prosperity did not make him forget that he owed everything to God. He had been trained in a Christian home, and he thought of himself as a Christian, though he had never made public profession of his faith in Christ.

Then came an incident that made him face life with new gravity. One day he was loading a wagon at the door of his father's store. He was called inside for a moment and another clerk took his place at the wagon. A moment later a pulley dropped on the head of the man who had come to his relief, and not many days after the man died from the effects of his injuries. William decided that he had been spared because there was work for him to do in the world; and he made the promise to serve God faithfully. That promise he never forgot.

When he was twenty years old the family moved to New York, William going also to take a position in his father's dry goods store. There were then one hundred and twenty thousand people in the city. Sixty years later, at a meeting of the leading business men of the city, he told of his life during the years of his clerkship. Among other interesting things, he said:

" I had to go every morning to Vanderwater Street for the keys, as my employers must have them in case of fire in the night. There was much ambition among the young men as to who should have his store opened first, and I used to be up soon after light, walk to Vanderwater Street and then to the store. It was to be sprinkled with water, which I brought the evening before from the old pump at the corner of Peck Slip and Pearl Street, then carefully swept and dusted. Then came sprinkling the sidewalk and street, and sweeping to the center a heap for the dirt cart to remove. This done, one of the older clerks would come and I would be permitted to go home for breakfast. In winter the wood was to be carried and piled in the cellar, fires were to be made, and lamps trimmed.

"When our employer would purchase a lot of goods at auction, it was our business to go and compare them with the bill. And if two of us could carry them home, we did so, as it would save the shilling porterage.

"Over the store in Pearl Street were a large number of boarding houses, expressly for country merchants. Here they would remain for a week or ten days, picking up a variety of goods, for most of them kept what were then called 'country' stores. It was a great object with the jobbers to have one of their salesmen board at a large house for country merchants, so that they could induce them to come to their stores to trade."

In 1827 the clerk started in business for himself. It was his intention to begin very modestly, using only the money he had saved. But a Connecticut merchant with whom he had done business, wishing to start his son in trade in New York, proposed that the two young men become partners, the father of the inexperienced man furnishing the larger part of the capital and promising to indorse for the firm to any reasonable amount.

Soon after the opening of the small store at 213 Pearl Street three young men entered, each carrying two large tin trunks suspended from straps over the shoulders. At once the senior member of the firm, recognizing them as Connecticut peddlers, proposed that they leave their trunks under the counter and make the store their headquarters, bringing their purchases there and packing their trunks in preparation for departure. They gladly accepted the offer, left their trunks, and went out. The junior partner objected to the presence of such unattractive looking men. But Mr. Dodge assured him that in time they would probably become men of mark, and good customers. He was a true prophet. One of the men after a few years became president of a New England bank; the second was long the leading man of an Ohio town, and the third became a Connecticut manufacturer. Each one bought large bills of goods during the six years the firm continued in business.

Mr. Dodge had prudently declared he would never marry until he was able to support a wife. The prosperity of the business made him feel that he could safely venture, so he asked Miss Melissa Phelps to be his wife. The wedding day was June 24, 1828, and the wedding journey was taken along Connecticut roads in a chaise built for two. From town to town they rode, stopping with friends by the way.

Mr. Phelps, the father of the bride, was the head of a great metal importing house. Four years after the marriage of his daughter, the new warehouse tumbled in ruins, owing to a defective foundation. The shock of the death of seven of his employees in the disaster unnerved him, and he longed for the strong hand of his son-in-law to take hold of the business with him. At first the idea did not appeal to the dry goods merchant, but he was even then learning to pay more heed to another's need of him than to his own dreams. So his business was sold, and he made the new venture. Phelps, Dodge and Company was the name of the new firm.

While in the dry goods business, Mr. Dodge had invested some of his savings in timber lands. His income from the new business was much larger, and he was able to increase his holdings. Later he invested in coal and iron lands, and was constant in his efforts for their development. Interested in every new demand for iron, he became an enthusiastic advocate of the Erie Railroad, and had much to do with securing the funds by which the road was built. He was long a director of the road, and also of the New Jersey Central Railroad, for whose construction he cut the first spadeful of soil in 1843. When the electric telegraph was successfully introduced, the following year, a large part of the credit was due to the far-sighted iron merchant.

Mr. Dodge made no secret of his desire to become wealthy; but his ambition was not allowed to interfere with his Christianity. He gave liberally of both time and money. Early in his business career he had begun to teach a Sunday-school class; and his interest in the members of the class never ended with Sunday. He followed them during the week, called on them in their homes or at business, and led them one by one into the Church. He took part in all sorts of activities that had as their object the benefit of his fellows. He was always faithful in his observance of Sunday. It is recorded that a companion on a trip to the South, who observed his unwillingness to travel on Sunday, united with the Church after returning to New York. Mr. Dodge's zeal for what he believed to be the right, had conquered him. On another trip South, Mr. and Mrs. Dodge reached a junction near Charleston, South Carolina, too late for the last Saturday night train; they had been delayed. Rather than travel on Sunday, they remained at the junction until Monday, and Mr. Dodge conducted services at the station. Wherever Sunday found him, there he sought a church and joined God's people in their worship. He never left his religion at home, but carried it with him wherever he went.

In his giving he was encouraged by the example of his partner, Mr. Phelps, who, as a young man, had known what the struggle with poverty meant.

It is recorded of him that the first twenty dollars he made he gave to another young man to help him in his education. When he began business he set apart sixty dollars from his first profits to buy an outfit for a missionary. Mr. Dodge had been a generous giver before he entered business with Mr. Phelps, but the encouragement of his partner and the enlarged income led him to increase his gifts. Many colleges were aided by him. His biographer well says that he might have endowed an institution to be named after him if he had chosen to lump his college gifts, but he felt that more good would be accomplished by the distribution in many directions. Another favourite benevolence was the partial support of young men who were studying for the ministry. For years there were never less than twenty on his list. Many appeals were made to him in behalf of young men already in college, but he preferred to confine his gifts to rather mature men who were struggling to enter the ministry without a college education.

Noting that the clerks in New York business houses had limited opportunities for reading, he was instrumental in founding and active in building up the Mercantile Library. He was interested from the first in the City Mission Society, a patron of the American Bible Society, and one of the founders of Union Theological Seminary. The list might be extended almost indefinitely. Even his most intimate friends found it impossible to make anything like a complete list of the institutions in which he was interested.

Wealth increased as the years passed. There were temporary losses; but as a rule the firm prospered in its undertakings. The country prospered, too, through the firm's activity. Ansonia, Connecticut, and Scranton, Pennsylvania, are two cities that owe a great deal to the house of Phelps, Dodge and Company. It is perhaps safe to say that if it had not been for Mr. Dodge and his influence, the brothers Scranton who founded the Pennsylvania city would have been unable to carry out their plans.

In 1861 Mr. Dodge withdrew from active connection with the firm, of which he had been the senior partner since the death of Mr. Phelps in 1853. To William E. Dodge, Jr., were committed many of the duties which had belonged to the father that Mr. Dodge might feel free to devote himself to the interests of the country, then on the verge of war. For years he had hoped that the war might be averted. But when he saw that it was inevitable, he prepared to serve the soldiers whom he had done so much to send to the front.

His opportunity came with the organization of the National Christian Commission, whose object was to relieve and care for the wounded, to conduct religious services in the army, and to supply reading matter and bodily comforts to the soldiers. Mr. Dodge associated himself with Mr. George H.

Stuart, of Philadelphia, President of the Commission, and during the four years of the war these men worked hand in hand.

Even more important was his unofficial service of his country. President Lincoln, Secretary Seward and Secretary Stanton, sought his counsel. Sometimes he was in Washington in conference with these leaders; again he was in Philadelphia, or Baltimore, or Chicago. Always he sought to advance his country's interests. When New York merchants were growing lukewarm in their zeal for the Union, he was depended on to spur them to new loyalty. When European sentiment was setting strongly against the North, to him was given the task of correcting the false impressions that were partly responsible for the injurious attitude. Though he was not an enlisted soldier, he played no mean part in the contest for the Union.

In the events that followed the war, he was to have an equally active part. He never sought public office, but in 1865 it was forced on him. While in Boston attending a meeting of the American Board of Commissioners of Foreign Missions, he received a telegram from New York notifying him of his nomination as Representative in Congress. He was elected by a decided majority; but his opponent, who had been Representative for some years, contested the seat. It was more than a year before the contest was decided in Mr. Dodge's favour.

In Washington the merchant-philanthropist was a marked man by reason of strong Christian principles. He became a regular attendant at the Congressional Prayer Meeting, where Senators and Representatives met to ask God's blessing on the nation. Soon he was looked upon as the strongest speaker at the meeting.

He was also strong as a speaker in the House. His ability to make an effective address was remarkable, as had been shown many times during the war. During his term important measures were considered, and his voice and vote were always on the side of the right as he saw it. The problems of reconstruction and temperance reform were among the subjects that interested him most. His record was so good that he was urged to accept a second nomination; but he declined.

The years that followed were not years of inactivity. He urged the selection of General Grant as President, was one of the leaders in the movement that brought about the union of Old School and New School bodies of the Presbyterian Church, and as treasurer of the fund raised to commemorate the union had much to do with the passing of eight million dollars into the treasury of the church. As a donor to Lincoln University, Pennsylvania, he did much for the education of the freedmen, and as one of the ten commissioners appointed by General Grant to manage Indian affairs, he helped to solve many of the problems presented by the neglected red men. When he resigned from the commission, he went to Georgia and helped to develop a section of that state by his wise investments in fir lands and the marketing of the product. In gratitude to him for his services the Georgia legislature named a new county in his honour.

The closing years of his life were full of activity for others and peace among his loved ones. In Dodge Hall, his New York home, he and Mrs. Dodge, who had been his helper through more than fifty years, welcomed hosts of friends who came there for guidance and counsel and for inspiration. Always they found him earnest, loyal and trustful, living in accordance with the stanza he was fond of quoting:

" Build a little fence of trust around to-day,
    Fill it full of useful works, and therein stay.
Look not through the sheltering bars upon to-morrow;
God will help thee bear what comes, of joy or sorrow."

When the end of life came suddenly, on February 8, 1883, thousands mourned, yet they rejoiced that they had known one of whom it was said: " A God-loving conscience was the tap root of his character; and the loss of such a conscience is a sorer bereavement to this community and the country than the loss of his bountiful purse."

William E. Dodge was a marvelously successful business man, but, as one who knew him has said, " his life represented, beyond everything else, the religion of the gospel."

II

From Carpenter's Apprentice to Philanthropist

The Story of Jacob Riis, Who Transformed New York's Tenement District

JACOB RIIS, the tenement house reformer and the friend of the children of the poor, laid the foundation for his interest in tenement houses very early in life in Ribe, Denmark, where he was born May 3, 1849. To be sure, his first experience was with a tenement for birds, not folks, but it was a tenement just the same. One of his first memories, he declared, was a starch box, placed by himself near his bedroom window, on the sunny side of the house. Very early in the spring there would be a great commotion in the box. The little Danish lad would watch eagerly then for he knew he would soon see his bird playmate, the starling, for whom the box was kept in the window. How the brothers and sisters of the household watched for " the glorious blue eggs," and how they welcomed the little starlings as, one by one, they broke their shells!

Some years later Jacob replaced the starch box with " a more substantial home, a tenement with

21

flats for three." Years afterward, when he "had
long been absorbed in the fight with tenements
made for human kind, by builders with no such
friendly feelings," his father wrote that the box
had been blown down, and that, within, was found
this note, written in a boyish hand:

> "This box is for starlings, not for sparrows.
>   "Jacob Riis."

The second tenement house experience came
when he was twelve or thirteen years old. The
most attractive spot in the town was a green hill,
but its beauty was marred for the boy by Rag Hall,
a ramshackle tenement "with shiftless tenants and
ragged children." Investigations had led him to
feel that the place must be made over. He was
fond of such investigations; he was known among
his companions as "Jacob the Delver," because he
was always looking into the whys and wherefors of
unpleasant things. One Christmas, when he had
received a present of a silver mark, he hurried to
Rag Hall, and proposed "to divide it with the
poorest family there, on the express condition that
they should tidy up things, especially their children,
and generally change their way of living. . . .
There really was some whitewashing done, and the
children were cleaned up for a season."

Ribe was an old town, of whose quaint customs
the enemy of tenement houses wrote many years
later in "The Old Town." One of the best pas-

sages in the book is that which tells of New Year
frolics:

" The old year went out with much such a racket
as we make nowadays, but of quite a different kind.
We did not blow the New Year in, we ' smashed '
it in. When it was dark on New Year's Eve, we
stole out with all the cracked and damaged crock-
ery of the year that had been hoarded for the purpose, and, hieing ourselves to some favourite
neighbour's door, broke our pots against it. Then
we ran, but not very far or very fast, for it was
part of the game that if one was caught at it, he
was to be taken in and treated to hot doughnuts.
The smashing was a mark of favour, and the
citizen who had most pots broken against his door
was the most popular man in town.

" When I was in the Latin school a cranky
burgomaster, whose door had been freshly painted,
gave orders to the watchmen to stop it, and gave
them an unhappy night, for they were hard put to
it to find a way it was safe to look, with the streets
full of the best citizens in town, and their wives
and daughters, sneaking singly by with bulging
coats on their way to salute a friend. Our mothers
baked more doughnuts than ever that night, and
beckoned the watchman in to the treat; and there
he sat, blissfully deaf while the street rang with the
thunderous salvos of our raids; until it was discovered that the burgomaster himself was on
patrol, when there was a sudden rush from kitchen

doors and a great scurrying through streets that grew strangely silent.

" The town had its revenge, however. The burgomaster, returning home in the midnight hours, stumbled at his gate over a discarded Christmas tree full of old boots and many black and sooty spots that went down around him with great smash in the street, so that his family came running out in alarm to find him sprawling in the midst of the biggest celebration of all. His dignity suffered a shock which he never got over quite. But it killed the New Year's fun, too. For he was really a good fellow, and then he was the burgomaster, and chief of police to boot. I suspect the fact was that the pot smashing had run its course. Perhaps the supply of pots was running out; we began to use tinware about that time."

The town watchman was a Ribe institution. He walked the streets and sang the hours. At ten he sang his good-night message, like this:

" Ho, watchman, heard ye the clock strike ten?
This hour is worth the knowing.
Ye households, high and low,
The time is here and going
When ye to bed should go;
Ask God to guard, and say amen.
  Be quick and bright—
  Watch fire and light,
Our clock just now struck ten."

At one o'clock he sang:

" Ho, watchman! Our clock is striking one.
O Jesus, wise and holy,
   Help us our cross to bear,
There is no one too lowly
   To be beneath thy care!
Our clock strikes one; in darkest night
   Oh, helpful Friend,
   Thy comfort send,
Then grows the burden light."

Jacob's father, who was in charge of the Latin form at the school, had fourteen children. He hoped to start all his sons on a professional career. Yet all but one of them disappointed him. Jacob, the third son, was destined for a literary life. But, to his father's great grief, the boy announced his determination to leave school. Mr. Riis pleaded with him; he wanted him to be either a school teacher or an author. But the boy was determined: he would be a carpenter. His father's warnings that this choice would take him out of the first class of the citizens of the town and make him a member of the despised third class, had no effect. His steadfastness to a purpose once formed, characteristic of him to the close of his life, was apparent then. Nothing would satisfy him but immediate apprenticeship to the town carpenter. Suppose his social position was lowered by the change? He would make a man of himself, and so win his place in the world.

He was fifteen when he first realized the change in his social position. One day, while on his way

home from the carpenter shop, he met a girl on the
bridge across the Nibs River. They had been children together, and he had seen her a thousand
times. But that day he saw her in a new light.
He knew that she was the girl he wanted, some
day, for his wife. Yet he knew that there was a
great gulf fixed between them, for she was the
daughter of the owner of the great factory in the
town, and he was the assistant of the carpenter
who was erecting a new building for the factory.
She lived at "The Castle," while he lived in a
cottage. How could he hope to win her? The
question did not bother him much. She must
be his wife, some day, somehow. He was heard
to say that he would marry her, or die in the
attempt. She learned of this, and he thought she
was offended.

He was then only thirteen years old; but he could
not take his eyes from her. "When she came
playing among the lumber where we were working,
danger dogged my steps," the lover wrote, years
after his marriage to the girl. "I carry a scar on
the shin bone, made with an adze I should have
been minding when I was looking after her. The
forefinger on my left hand has a stiff joint. I cut
that off with an axe when she was dancing on a
beam close by. Though it was put on again by a
clever surgeon and kept on, I have never had the
use of it since. But what did a finger matter, or
ten, if Elizabeth was only there! Once I fell off

the roof where I must crane my neck to see her go
around the corner."

It was his love for Elizabeth that drove him
from Ribe. He joined a dancing class to be near
her. At the ball which closed the term he was floor
committee, and he took it upon himself to order
from the floor Elizabeth's father, who violated the
rule that no adult was allowed to dance before
midnight. The scandal that followed led him to go
to Copenhagen to finish his apprenticeship with a
great builder. Within three days of his arrival in
the city he had an adventure. A stranger, who
observed his uncertainty when he was trying to
find his way in the new surroundings, offered to
help him. They walked on together, and in a short
time became great friends. Soon Jacob told him
that he liked Copenhagen very much, because
everyone was so friendly. Just then they were at
the palace door; the lackey who stood before it
bowed low. Jacob declared this an example of the
friendliness to strangers of which he had just
spoken, for he had never seen the lackey before.
What was his astonishment to learn later that the
stranger was King Christian, and that the lackey
was bowing to his royal master. Years later, when
Mr. Riis visited the palace, as a friend of the King,
the relating of the story was a cause of much
amusement.

When Jacob had served his apprenticeship, he
took steerage passage for America, resolved to win

his way to fame and fortune. He had his trade, and he had several letters of introduction. But the men to whom these were written were absent in Europe, and he realized that he was friendless in a great city. Soon he started·to Pittsburgh with a party of men who had agreed to work in a blast furnace. For a little while he served as a carpenter on laborers' houses, and then, boylike, he quit on the spur of the moment when he learned that France and Prussia were at war, and that Denmark would probably fight with Prussia. Reaching New York, he offered his services to the Danish consul. Receiving no favorable word, however, he was soon near starvation, for when he reached the city he had only one cent in his pocket. The story of the next weeks is pitiful. He visited the pawnshop, slept in a milk wagon, was given a meal by the roadside, hoed cucumbers for three days and slept in fields and barns after his hoeing was finished. Then he tried work in a claybank and in a brickyard. Sometimes, when he was out of work, he slept in doorways, wrapped in the blanket which his mother had put in his trunk when he left home.

At this period he made his first acquaintance with the East Side tenements, against which he was soon to begin a bitter warfare. In " The Making of an American," he told this incident of that time:

" One rainy night in late October I sat—cold and wet and hungry—on the bank of the North River.

I was discouraged; a thought of suicide was in my mind. Just then a wretched dog crept up to me. I felt its cold body against my leg. It was the dog which had been my companion for many nights of doorway-sleeping. Dog-fashion, it climbed upon me and licked my face. The love of the faithful little beast thawed the icicles of my heart. I picked it up in my arms and fled from the tempter.

"At midnight, the comrades—dog and boy— entered the police station where lodging was given to homeless men. As the rules forbade the entrance of dogs, the Danish wanderer put the dog under his coat. It was seen, however, and put out of the door. During the night the gold locket on my neck—containing home relics—was stolen. I complained, and was thrown out of the station without ceremony. The dog, seeing his master abused, leaped upon the doorman, who immediately grabbed the animal and brutally killed him."

Years passed. The memory of the murder of his dog rankled. Finally, through his influence at police headquarters, gained by fearless work as reporter on the *Tribune,* he felt he could crush the sergeant who had been responsible for the great wrong of that October night. Who was he? He would learn. All he had to do was to examine the blotter of that police station for October, 1870. He went to the station for the purpose. But he could not look. Again and again he went, only to leave the information still locked within the records.

Once he went so far as to take the blotter in his hands. But, before he opened it, he saw the way to a nobler revenge than the discharge of the sergeant. He would let the sergeant alone; he was only the creature of an institution which was working great wrong—the station lodging-houses, breeding-places of crime. He would give the death blow to these lodging-houses, with all their misery. He interested Theodore Roosevelt, then police commissioner, in his cause, and the stations were closed to tramps. The city was benefited, and Jacob Riis had conquered himself.

During all the years of his life in New York City Jacob Riis was the helper of the poor. As police reporter for " The New York Sun," he came in touch with misery that he longed to alleviate. He felt that the best way to do this was to change living conditions. So he fought the old fashioned tenements and at last succeeded in making illegal the erection of further structures like those that long disgraced the city. He led a crusade that resulted in the demolition of many of the old buildings, and the substitution of a small park at one of the most overcrowded spots in the city. He prevailed on the board of education to equip playgrounds for the children of the tenements, and he led in the crusade for modern school buildings in the neglected sections of the city. He made a campaign against cheap lodging houses. He was always the friend of the unfortunate.

His own home he made in a beautiful spot on Long Island. When he came to the city in the morning he tried to take with him some of its brightness for the children of the poor. But he did not learn how to do this until he was shown the way by his own children. In " The Making of an American," he told how these children taught him a lesson in real philanthropy.

In the spring his children roamed at will through the woods and the meadows. As they enjoyed the freedom of the fields and the beauty of the flowers and the trees, they thought with pity of the children in the city, of whom they had heard their father speak.

So one day they filled their arms with daisies, and took them to him, just as he was starting for the city. These they asked him to take to " the poors."

" I did as they bade me," wrote Mr. Riis, " but I did not get more than a block from the ferry with my burden. The street children went wild over the ' posies.' They pleaded and fought to get near me, and when I had no flowers to give them sat in the gutter and wept with grief."

The sight so affected Mr. Riis that he wrote a letter to the papers, calling the attention of the thousands who daily leave their homes in the country for city shops and offices to their opportunity for bringing joy to the hearts of other thousands by carrying to them a bit of the country. In concluding, he promised that all flowers sent to his city address would be carefully distributed.

The result of the appeal was surprising. " Flowers came pouring in from every corner of the compass. They came in boxes, in barrels, and in bunches, from field and garden, from town and country. Express wagons carrying flowers jammed Mulberry Street, and the police came out to marvel at the row. The office was fairly smothered in fragrance. A howling mob of children besieged it.

" The reporters forgot their rivalries and lent a hand with enthusiasm in giving out the flowers. The superintendent of police detailed five stout patrolmen to help carry the abundance to points of convenient distribution.

" Fretful babies stopped crying and smiled as the messengers of love were laid against their wan cheeks. Slovenly women courtesied and made way. The Italians in the Barracks stopped quarrelling to keep order. The worst street became suddenly quiet and neighbourly."

One of the boxes of flowers was sent in by a New Jersey circle of King's Daughters. This gave Mr. Riis an idea: he would interest the King's Daughters in a work which threatened to become too large for his time and strength. So he appealed to them at a public meeting.

The appeal was not in vain. The King's Daughters undertook the work, and opened a basement office. Soon they saw an opportunity to extend their work. The Board of Health every summer sent fifty doctors to canvass the city's thirty thousand tenements and prescribe for the sick poor. It was possible thus to reach each family once and only once, and the visitation thus failed of much which might have been accomplished.

The King's Daughters determined to follow up the physicians with a nurse, whose duty it was to take to the poor the things the doctors could not give, " advice, instruction, a friendly lift out of a hopeless rut."

At the end of the first season the King's Daughters found it impossible to abandon the work for the winter. So two rooms were rented in a tenement. From these the labour of love was continued. Later two houses were secured for the work.

And thus, at last, an effective way was found to reach the hearts of the dwellers in the tenements. " It was like cutting windows for souls that were being shrunk and dwarfed in their mean setting," was Mr. Riis's striking comment on the work of the Settlement.

Having learned the secret of reaching the poor effectively, Mr. Riis went on, until his death in 1915, in his self-imposed work of lightening the burdens of those whom he called " the other half." And when the history of American philanthropy is written, his name must be given prominent place.

III

A Modest Man's Conquest

How J. Marion Sims Became the First Surgeon of His Generation

ONE hundred years ago schools were scarce in South Carolina, so the parents of J. Marion Sims were compelled to choose a boarding-school six or eight miles from home. The boy, who was born on January 25, 1813, was only six years old when he was enrolled there. During his six months' experience at school he saw his father but once, though his mother came to see him every month.

But the separation from home folks was not the most trying thing about the school. The master was a brute. It was his invariable habit to whip every newcomer on the day of his appearance, and the younger the boy the harder would be the whipping. No matter how good the boy was the teacher was sure to find a pretext. Always the whipping continued till the child was completely exhausted.

After enduring the brutality of the master as long as he could, the lad begged his mother, on the occasion of one of her visits, to be allowed to return home with her. He tried to speak to her

34

alone, but the master would not permit them to be by themselves. So he told his story in the presence of the tyrant. Mrs. Sims pleaded with her husband to grant the boy's request. He was reluctant to interrupt his son's schooling. He himself had not been allowed to attend school a single day during his own boyhood; his education had been secured after his marriage. But he could not withstand the pleadings of Marion and his mother, so the boy was recalled.

When Marion was twelve years old his father moved to Lancaster, South Carolina, in order that he might send his children to a classical preparatory school. The boy told his father that he thought he ought to go into a store and so help in the support of the family of eight children. But Mr. Sims' heart was set on giving his children a better chance than he had enjoyed, and he turned a deaf ear to all entreaties. When the boy was ready for college, he renewed his appeals, but his father, who hoped to see his son practicing law, was determined that the boy's education should be continued.

Marion made one more effort before he finally decided that his father must be allowed to have his way. Six months after entering the sophomore class of the College of South Carolina, at Columbia, he determined to go home, unannounced, secure a position in a store, and become an income-producer for the large family. When he reached home his father was absent. He told his plan to his mother, but she promptly explained to him the impossibility of his leaving college when his father's heart was set on his graduation. She let him know that she also had her dreams for his future; she wished above all things to see him a Presbyterian minister. Heartily ashamed of himself, he hurried back to Columbia.

Many of the students were sons of wealthy planters, and their habits were not always the best. On several occasions they tried to lead Marion into mischief. They were particularly anxious to make him a companion in their drinking bouts. Twice he gave way to their pleas, but after sorrowful experience of the results of his lapses, he decided to take a brave stand. So he said to his tempters:

" See here, boys, you can all drink, and I can not. You like wine and I do not. I hate it; its taste is disagreeable. Its effects are dreadful, because it makes me drunk. Now, I hope you all will understand the position I occupy. I don't think it is right for you to ask me to drink wine when I don't want it, and it produces such a bad effect upon me."

His heart was heavy as Commencement Day approached, not because he must leave college, but because he felt he must disappoint both his father and his mother by telling them that he had determined to be a doctor. He was not attracted by medicine, but it was a recognized thing that a college graduate was shut up to the three learned professions. He would not be a minister, and he could not be a lawyer, so he must be a doctor. His mother was spared the disclosure he dreaded to make, as she died two months before his graduation.

When he told his father his plans, Mr. Sims showed his bitter disappointment, in words that were hardly calculated to add to the attraction of medicine in his son's eye:

" Well, I suppose that I cannot control you; but it is a profession for which I have the utmost contempt. There is no science in it. There is no honour to be achieved in it; no reputation to be made. And to think that *my* son should be going around from house to house, through this country, with a box of pills in one hand, and a squirt in the other, to ameliorate human suffering, is a thought I never supposed I should have to contemplate."

Notwithstanding his disappointment, Mr. Sims gave his son the best opportunity to study for his chosen profession. First in Charlotte, then in Philadelphia, the young man attended medical college. His excessive timidity was a drawback in both places. He was slight and short; he had no confidence in himself; and the feeling that he was planning for a professional life in opposition to his father's wishes added to his hesitation to begin work. At the close of his course he put off the evil day of beginning practice by taking a special course offered by one of the professors. He knew that he was a skilful surgeon, but he felt that he would never shine as a general practitioner.

At last he nerved himself to announce to the citizens of his home town his readiness to serve them. A tin sign was tacked to the front of his office. In later life he laughed at the size of the sign; it was at least two feet wide, and stretched at least one-third of the way across the front of the office. In this office he displayed his set of surgical instruments, his stock of medicine, and his library of seven volumes, and waited for patients.

At the end of two weeks one of the leading men of the town asked him to attend his baby. He took a good look at the child, but had not the least idea what to do. Returning to his office he copied from one of his books a prescription that might suit the baby's need, prepared the medicine, and sent it to the house. When the next visit showed no improvement, he tried a second prescription, secured in the same way. A few days later the child died, and he was utterly cast down. He felt that his days of usefulness were done before they had begun.

Two weeks later he had his second chance. He was asked to treat a second baby, sick of the same disease as the first patient. Again he had no confidence in his own judgment, but gave the child exactly the same medicine as he had given before, merely reversing the order of the prescriptions. The result was the same: the child died.

"I went home sadder than ever," the young doctor told the story of that black day. "I just took the long tin sign-board from my office door. There was an old well back of the house, covered over with boards. I went to the well, took that sign with me, dropped it in there, and covered the old well over again. I was no longer a doctor in the town of Lancaster. If I had had money enough, or any money at all, I would not have given another dose of medicine. But there was no alternative for me. Being obliged to continue in the profession that I had started in, I was determined to make up my deficiency by hard work; and this was not to come from reading books, but from observation and from diligent attention to the sick."

On October 13, 1835, he started in search of a new field. It was always his delight to show his lack of faith in popular superstitions by choosing Friday or the thirteenth day of the month for important events. In later years, when each of four surgeons in the Woman's Hospital of New York, was choosing his weekly operating day, Dr. Sims set them at rest by choosing Friday. They made no objection.

The journey from Lancaster was made in a little carry-all in which had been packed medicine, instruments, and his library of seven volumes. After three weeks he reached Mount Meigs, Alabama. There he gave his note for two hundred dollars for the books and medicines of a physician who was giving up practice. The physician recommended the young man to his patients, and once more prospects seemed bright.

But, as before, lack of self-confidence was a barrier. His first invitation was to consult with the physician attending the daughter of a wealthy family. To this he responded:

" No, I cannot go; you want an older man than I am, and a man with experience. I haven't the knowledge that will satisfy the case and I think that you had better go to Montgomery and get one of the swell doctors to attend to the case."

Not until the messenger urged him repeatedly did he consent to go to the patient. Of his reception Dr. Sims has said:

" The father was glad to see me, and welcomed me as if I had been a real doctor. Though I was twenty-two years old, I had no beard, and looked like a boy."

He conducted himself so wisely that both the attending physician and the family were pleased. The father suggested that he go to see a sick man in the neighborhood whom many physicians had tried to benefit, but in vain. He answered that he really preferred not to go; that some big doctor had better take the case.

" He won't care to see me," he said. " I haven't the knowledge and reputation sufficient to take the charge of such a case as that. It has baffled the skill of all the doctors, and I have no desire to undertake anything that I know so little about."

At last he consented to go, but when he came into the presence of the sick man his lack of confidence must have been apparent, for the first words he heard were:

"Do you call that thing a doctor? Take him away. I have got no use for such a looking man as that. I am too sick a man to be fooled with. Take him away."

"I haven't the least desire to prescribe for you," Dr. Sims responded. "I have great sympathy for you, and for everybody else who is sick, and I want to see them all get well. I haven't the knowledge or experience necessary to treat any man who is as sick as you are, or as you seem to be."

Quieted by the words, the patient talked fully of his symptoms. Then the doctor rode away.

A month passed. Eight or nine different physicians visited the patient and were unable to do anything for him. Then Dr. Sims was sent for once more. Fearfully he diagnosed the case, and said that an operation must be performed. There was objection, but he insisted. Another physician was called in consultation, and he disagreed with the proposed treatment. Opposition was the one thing needed to bring out Dr. Sims' self-assertion. He insisted that he was right; he knew his ground. At last he was given his way. The issue proved that he was correct. The patient made a rapid recovery, and Dr. Sims' fame speedily went abroad through that region. But, best of all, the young doctor had gained what he most needed, self-assertion, self-mastery, self-confidence.

Prosperity came to him as a result of finding himself. In a few months he felt he could offer a home to the woman who had promised to marry him, and he went back to South Carolina for her. After their marriage he continued in quiet country practice, but he never fell in love with his profession. In 1838, when a Philadelphia friend asked him to go into partnership with him in a clothing store at Vicksburg, Mississippi, he consented, sold his home, and made all his arrangements to move. Then the bottom fell out of his friend's prospects, and he was adrift. But he re-opened his office, and within two years was earning three thousand dollars a year. Then a friend urged him to go elsewhere, that both prospects and health might be improved. When he suggested that he move to Montgomery, the old self-distrust manifested itself:

" That is impossible. I am nothing but a little country doctor, from the pine woods, with no money and no reputation to start me, and a family of children dependent on me, and I must go to some place where it would be easier to get practice, and where people would be obliged to employ me, whether they wished or not."

But Mrs. Sims, whose advice her husband had

learned to value, urged him to go to Montgomery. She knew his capability better than he did. Within five years her judgment was vindicated. He was the best-known practitioner in the city, and was especially famous for his successful surgical operations for various malformations.

The turning point in his life came when he treated a country patient for a trying deformity. He was so wonderfully successful in this that he was urged by a doctor to write an account for the *Journal of Dental Surgery*. He insisted that he could not write.

" I should be ashamed to see anything of mine in print," he said. " I cannot write. I never wrote anything in my life. It is not my forte."

The plea of his visitor prevailed, however, and the article was written and published. He read the printed article and was so ashamed of it that he hid it behind a large volume in his library. It was his fear that one of his fellow-practitioners might see it and make sport of him.

Not long after this, one of the very physicians whose ridicule of the article he most dreaded entered his office, went to the bookcase, and began turning over the books. On withdrawing one volume, he saw a magazine behind it and drew it out. Dr. Sims was quaking. The visitor opened the pages, and began to read the awful article.

" I was trembling like a leaf," Dr. Sims said later, " as I stood there like a schoolboy. He did not look up at all, or say a word, but stood there, reading it down the first page, and then on the second page. It just occupied two pages. My heart was in my throat. As he finished the article he stood perfectly still, and I also stood perfectly still, trembling. As he turned around I thought, ' I shall get it now.' "

But the visiting physician said: " What would I give if I had the faculty of expressing myself in writing like that! I have never read a thing so natural in my life as your description of the case. I have seen you perform many beautiful operations and many difficult ones, and I advise you to report them for the press. Seeing that you are so timid, and lack confidence in yourself, if you will send your productions to me, I shall be very glad to make such suggestions as are necessary."

That was the beginning of literary activity that brought deserved fame to the young surgeon, and increased his confidence in himself. Gratefully he wrote, in 1883:

" Even to this day the finding of that Dental Journal is inexplicable to me. I do not believe there are any accidents in this world. I do not look upon that as an accident, but as a Providential affair."

This belief in an overruling Providence was one great secret of the marvelous success that came to him during the remaining thirty-eight years of his life.

In 1853 he formed the daring plan of going to New York. He had been in poor health, and experience in the North showed him that he needed a cooler climate. Encouraged by Mrs. Sims, he moved to the metropolis. There he had many difficulties, and he had need of all the self-confidence he had acquired. Physicians did not welcome him. He began to dream of a women's hospital, where he might practice. Finally, when funds were reduced to one hundred and sixteen dollars, Dr. Sims proposed to return to Alabama. Mrs. Sims would not listen to him, but said she knew he would eventually succeed; that she had an abiding confidence in God.

After a most trying year better days came. Through the influence of powerful friends the Women's Hospital was founded, and Dr. Sims had the opportunity to give to New York sufferers the benefit of his important discoveries.

Then came years of successful ministering to the suffering of New York, London and Paris. He was honoured by his colleagues as the greatest surgeon of his day, he was decorated by five governments of Europe, and when he died, on Nov. 13, 1883, the scientific world united in honouring his memory. One famous man declared that if all Dr. Sims' discoveries were suppressed, it would be found that his own peculiar branch of surgery had gone backward at least twenty-five years.

IV

The Inventor of Shorthand

How Isaac Pitman Prepared Himself for His Task

"ISAAC PITMAN, born Jan. 4, 1813," was
the record written by the father, Samuel
Pitman, in the center of the horoscope prepared for the baby according to the so-called
science of astrology. This was duly inscribed in
the family Bible, and was consulted many times by
those who would know Isaac's future. The prophecies were varied, but it did not occur to anyone to
declare the one thing which was to bring fame to
the Pitman name through him whose future was
supposed to be determined by the constellations
that were in the ascendant at the moment of his
birth. It is recorded that his father later aban-
doned his belief in astrology, perhaps because of its
failure in the case of his son.

Mr. Pitman was one of the early friends of
popular education in England, and he was among
those responsible for the opening of a parochial
school at Trowbridge, which was attended by
Isaac. The boy's stay there was not lengthy. He
was subject to fainting fits, and when he was
thirteen years old it was thought best to take him

out of school. Although the fainting boy speedily recovered his senses when taken into the open air, no one stopped to think that the attacks were not due to physical weakness, but to a miserably ventilated school-room. In that day no one realized the need for fresh air. One hundred boys were crowded into a room twenty-five by fifteen feet and eight or nine feet high.

During the excursions into the fresh air made necessary by his " weakness," Isaac made the acquaintance of the church yard, which was the playground of his schoolmates. He did not join them in their sports there or anywhere else, as even when very young he seemed to think he was in the world for something more serious than play. His brother Jacob once said of him: " Isaac never had any of that rollicking nonsense about him peculiar to most of us boys, nor do I remember his ever stopping on his way from school to play, but home directly he went, either to his books or to his work." Thus he did not share the strapping which was the recognized penalty in the Pitman home for loitering on the streets. Yet he took part with his brothers in the sports of walking, bathing and swimming, which parental edict made a part of the routine for the family.

When he left school Isaac became a junior clerk in the counting-house of a village cloth manufacturer. While he liked the work, he was not satisfied to think that his education was finished, and he begged for an opportunity to return to school. When his request was refused, he determined to study at home. The long office hours, from six in the morning to six at night, made study difficult, but he showed conclusively that where there is a will there is a way, and that he had the will. He was accustomed to leave his bed at four, in order that he might study two hours before the beginning of the day's work. Two hours in the evening also were set apart for study. Sometimes it happened that work at the factory was light, and the young clerk was excused for the morning. Instead of taking the time for sport, it was his habit to carry a book with him into the fields or under the trees.

" One of the books which he made his companion in morning walks into the country was ' Lennie's Grammar,' " writes Thomas Allen Reid, in his biography of Pitman. " The conjugation of verbs, lists of irregular verbs, adverbs, prepositions, and conjunctions, and the thirty-six rules of syntax, he committed to memory so that he could repeat them in order. The study of the book gave him a transparent English style."

There was a local library to which his father subscribed, one of the earliest lending libraries in the country, and Isaac was one of its most diligent readers. " I went regularly to the library for fresh supplies of books," Isaac said, in 1868, " and thus read most of the English classics. I think I was

quite as familiar with Addison and Sir Roger, and
Will Honeycomb, and all the club, as I was with
my own brothers and sisters. . . . and when reading the ' Spectator ' at that early age, I wished that
I might be able to do something in letters."

Before he left school he formed the habit of
copying choice pieces of poetry and prose into a
little book which he kept in his pocket. These he
would commit to memory when he had leisure.
" Two of these little pocket albums have been preserved," Mr. Reid writes. " One contains extracts
from Pope, Milton, Cowper, James Montgomery,
the Psalms, and Isaiah, interspersed with the Greek
alphabet, the Signs of the Zodiac, arithmetical
tables, and other items of useful information.
The book is dated May 31, 1825. The penman-
ship is extremely neat and distinct. A later
pocket companion contains a neatly written copy
of Valpey's Greek Grammar, as far as the syntax,
which he committed to memory; a chronological
table, etc. In his morning walks in 1832 he
committed to memory the first fourteen chapters
of Proverbs. He would not undertake a fresh
chapter until he had repeated the preceding one
without hesitation."

As most of his knowledge of words was gained
from books he had difficulty in pronunciation. A
large portion of the language of books he had
never heard in conversation, or at school, and the
misleading or ambiguous spelling of these words

often led him to pronounce them (mentally) inaccurately. His method of overcoming this deficiency was ingenious. Again and again he read " Paradise Lost." Careful attention to the meter enabled him to correct his faulty pronunciation of many words. Words not found in the poem he discovered in the dictionary. With unusual courage he decided to read through Walker's Dictionary, fixing his mind on words new to him and on the spelling and pronunciation of familiar terms. On the pages of one of his pocket-books he copied all words he had been in the habit of mispronouncing. " They numbered about two thousand, and their correct pronunciation had to be fixed in the memory by repetition." He was seventeen when the dictionary plan was carried out completely. Two years later he reviewed this book.

The labor of writing out so many extracts from books led him to take an interest in the imperfect system of shorthand then current. Longing to be able to divide his labor by six, he borrowed an instruction book, copied the alphabet and word signs, made these his own, and began the writing of shorthand, which he continued through life.

When he was eighteen years old he left the counting-house to attend a training school for teachers. Five months' instruction was sufficient to prepare him to take charge of his first school. Such a good impression was made by him on his instructors that when his father applied for the admission of another of his eleven children, the Head Master told him he might send as many more of his children as he could spare.

When young Pitman alighted from the stage-coach at Barton-on-Humber, where he was under appointment to teach, he was possessed of three half crowns, about one dollar and eighty cents. But he was resolved to care for himself and to save money out of his small salary. This he was able to do, his exactness in keeping accounts, his promptness in paying his bills, and his readiness to give away a portion of his receipts, being factors that helped him in carrying out his resolution.

Although he had one hundred and twenty boys in his school, he was not satisfied to devote all his time to them. He did his school work thoroughly, and then had time for other employments. He lectured on astronomy in the village, and made other efforts to improve the people who were too old to attend his school. He threw himself ardently into the fight for temperance reform. But the greatest of his outside activities was his service as a local preacher at the Methodist chapel at Ulceby.

Little is known of his work as a preacher except the fact that at Ulceby he became acquainted with Bagster's " Comprehensive Bible." This is important because it was the turning point of his life. Having noted many errors in the references given in the copy of the Bible he had been accustomed to use, he was curious to see if the new edition was more accurate. He soon found that, while the Bagster Bible was an improvement on the edition he had used, there were some mistakes in the references. So he wrote to the publisher, Samuel Bagster, on October 15, 1835:

"I have made it my custom for two or three years in my morning and evening reading of Scripture, to refer to every parallel place; in some measure appreciating the value of the plan. If you would like to place a copy of your Bible under my care, to be considered your property, I would make a constant and careful use of it, and give you the benefit of the corrections and mistakes which I might discover in reading it through."

The publisher, glad to accept the offer of his unknown correspondent, at once sent him the copy requested. Pitman promptly mapped out the work he had undertaken. He found there were five hundred thousand references, each one of which was to be verified carefully. He decided that it would be possible to complete the revision in three years.

For convenience, the Bible was divided into seven parts, and at the conclusion of each part a statement of errors discovered was sent to Mr. Bagster. The publisher was so delighted with the results that he begged his volunteer assistant to set any price he chose on his work, and said that this would gladly be paid. But Mr. Pitman had undertaken the task as a labour of love, and he would not listen to any suggestion of compensation. Although five thousand hours of close study were required to complete the work as planned, the schoolmaster-preacher persisted in declining to receive payment. When the final errors discovered were corrected in a new edition of the Bible, Mr. Bagster sent him a beautifully bound copy. A silver plate on the cover told of the invaluable services of the man to whom the Bible was given.

Most of this work on the Bible was done at Wotton-under-Edge, where Mr. Pitman conducted his second school. As in the first school, his work was most successful, but he was compelled to resign because of dissatisfaction with his changed religious views. He had become a disciple of Swedenborg, and neither the School Board nor the Wesleyan authorities were willing to put up with his new ideas.

At once Mr. Pitman opened a private school in the same town, and soon was enjoying a larger income than before. His school became popular partly because of its introduction of shorthand as one of the subjects of instruction. The system of Samuel Taylor, which Pitman had learned as a boy, was the basis of teaching. Before long he made up his mind that a cheaper manual than any in the market must be prepared if, as he hoped, the system was to be made a part of the curriculum of all the schools in the country. Accordingly he prepared the manual which he desired to have published for threepence, and submitted it to Mr. Bagster, whose friendship he had won by his work on the Bible. Mr. Bagster, advised by a reporter to whom he submitted the manuscript of the proposed manual, suggested that Mr. Pitman should compile a new system. This suggestion was a surprise. " I had no intention of becoming a shorthand author," the schoolmaster wrote. " The ambition of appearing before the public in that manner never entered my mind until it was suggested to me as a means of accomplishing an end."

From that time every spare moment was devoted to devising the new system. As he walked to and from school, at intervals between engagements, even during brief holidays, he was thinking of signs and shadings and hooks and vowel signs and word signs. It was his purpose to make the system phonetic, based on his study of the sounds of English words, accomplished years before by the aid of Walker's Dictionary.

On November 15, 1837, the first edition of " Stenograph Sound-Hand by Isaac Pitman," was put on sale in London. The plates had been made under the author's direction. The modest manual consisted of twelve pages and two plates, enclosed in a drab cover of thin cardboard. The binding was done by the older boys in the author's school, who were delighted to do what seemed to them half-play. The first two hundred copies were so poorly done that Mr. Pitman called in a stationer to instruct the amateurs. He did not have to apologize for the work done on the remainder of the edition.

The reception of the new system was cordial. The fact that such a well-known publisher as Samuel Bagster issued the book was a help in advertising it, but as soon as the people became acquainted with the merits of the invention of Pitman, it needed no advertisement.

In 1839 the author removed to Bath, where he opened a new school. The prospectus stated that the master's new system of writing by sound would be taught. This was the beginning of the Phonetic Institute which for many years was a Bath institution.

Improved editions of the system which had already made the name of Isaac Pitman famous followed within the next four or five years. Perhaps the most helpful of these was the " Penny Plate," in which the principles of the system were presented in brief compass. This was issued in 1840, when Penny Postage promised to work great transformations. On this plate the offer was made by Mr. Pitman that he would correspond with anyone about the system, correcting their exercise papers and helping them in any way he could; for this service he would make no charge. In this way, as well as by giving free lectures on his system, far and near, he hoped to popularize it. His thought was not to reap a fortune by his invention, but to make life easier for hundreds of thousands. The measure of the public appreciation of his efforts is apparent from these lines, written at the time:

    " Artists and scribes no more delight,
      Their arts imperfect found;
     Daguerre now draws by rays of light,
      And Pitman writes by Sound."

On May 21, 1894, Mr. Pitman was knighted by Queen Victoria, in recognition of his services of more than half a century to Stenography, and the great utility of the art.

Three years later, on January 22, 1897, his life on earth ended. One of his last acts was to leave in the hands of a friend this message:

" To those who ask how Isaac Pitman passed away, say, ' Peacefully, and with no more concern than in passing from one room into another to take up some further employment.' "

V

Out of An Indian Tepee

The Wonderful Story of Charles A. Eastman

ONE of the best known of the full-blood Indians who have risen from savagery to a position of leadership on an equality with their white neighbors is Charles A. Eastman, who was born in the lodge of Many Lightnings, a Santee Sioux, in 1858. He has told the story of the first fifteen years of his life in " An Indian Boyhood," which is not only a bit of autobiography but, as well, a stirring and authentic picture of child life in the camps of the American red man.

When Charles Eastman was a lad he had a different name. In fact, he has borne several names, as is customary among his people. His first name was " Hakadah," or " The Pitiful Last," suggested by the death of his mother when he was yet quite young. This name was retained until, as the reward of prowess, another designation became his.

Uncheedah, the grandmother, took the motherless boy and strapped him to the board which, for months, was to be his bed. To the sides of this board a beautiful sack was nailed, which was tightly laced over the body of the pappoose. Thus

he was ready to be carried on the back, laid on the
floor, hung from the branch of a tree, or tilted
against the lodge-pole. He gave little trouble. At
night he usually slept well, but when he had to be
quieted Uncheedah would sing:

" Sleep, sleep, my boy, the Chippewas
    Are far away—are far away.
Sleep, sleep, my boy; prepare to meet
    The foe by day—the foe by day.
The cowards will not dare to fight
    Till morning break—till morning break.
Sleep, sleep, my child, while still 'tis night;
    Then bravely wake—then bravely wake."

Before he left his primitive cradle, Hakadah
made friends with the squirrels and the birds.
And as soon as he could walk he knew Shechoka
(the robin), Oopehanska (the thrush), Hinakaga
(the owl), and many of the other feathered inhab-
itants of the forest.

At an early age he had his first experiences as a
traveler. He thought it great fun to be placed in
the dog-travaux, lodge-poles fastened together and
dragged by dogs. Sometimes he was put on a
horse's back in one of two sacks fastened together
after the manner of saddle-bags. Another child
was in the second sack. On one occasion, when a
little girl was his sack-companion, the horse lay
down in a snowdrift. He remembered that ride, as
also his first experience in a wagon with wheels.
When the wagon was moving rapidly he innocently

stepped from the bed to the rear wheel, and was much astonished when he found himself in the road with the wheel on his body. The man who drove the wagon which followed close afterward checked his team quickly, or the experimenter with a strange vehicle would have been severely injured. Instead of blaming himself, he blamed the white man's wagon, and rejoiced when it was left behind and he was safe once more in the dog-travaux. This was the conveyance he enjoyed most. He describes it in his book as " a set of rawhide strips securely lashed to the tent poles, which were harnessed to the sides of the animal as if he stood between shafts, while the free ends were allowed to drag on the ground." Sometimes ponies were used instead of dogs. The small children were loaded on the travaux with the baggage.

A trying adventure in a far less trustworthy vehicle came not long after the wagon experience. Soldiers were in the field because of the depredations of certain Indians, and the company to which Hakadah belonged fled in terror across the Missouri. They knew that the stream was treacherous even when skilled oarsmen used a staunch boat. But they were able to secure only buffalo skin boats, as round as tubs! " The women and the old men made and equipped the temporary boats, braced with ribs of willow. Some of these were towed by two or three women or men swimming in the water and some by ponies." It was difficult to keep them from capsizing. But these bold navigators did their best, for in the boats of skin were the children and all their valuables. So dangerous were these boats that more than once Hakadah's grandmother, who was nearly seventy years old, preferred to swim across swift streams, bearing the boy on her shoulders, rather than trust him to the skins.

When the shore was reached, the children were strapped in the saddles or held in front of an older person. As the fugitives traveled by night as well as by day, all suffered for lack of sleep and food. " Meals were eaten hastily, and sometimes in the saddle. Water was not always to be found. The people carried it with them in bags formed of tripe or the dried pericardium of animals."

Hakadah's first experience with a prairie fire was startling. Scorching flame and blinding, choking smoke seemed to make escape impossible. But Indian craft saved the party. A back fire was made, and all escaped. Only a few months later a danger of an entirely different character threatened him and all his party. A blizzard of unusual severity overtook them. There was nothing to do but lie down in sheltered spots and permit the snow to drift over them. Warm and dry in their wintry beds, all were quite content until the men announced that the storm was over. When they had dug their way out, they found a herd of buffaloes and were able to satisfy their hunger.

But food was not always at hand when needed. One spring Hakadah learned what hunger meant. For days he had nothing to eat. Then, one morning, there was food—six small birds for six large families. One wing was his share. How hungry he was that day! But the pain was speedily forgotten when the hunters returned with choice morsels from many buffaloes. Then what a feast there was in the camp!

Even when food was plentiful Hakadah did not always have his fill. He was taught to fast, in order that he might be ready for the hardships of travel or famine. Another feature of his training which made a deep impression on him was the daily exercise prescribed for all members of the tribe, for they must be ready at any moment to make a forced march, or to carry such a heavy burden as a deer killed far from camp. To the women was committed the carrying of the more commonplace baggage, as it was beneath the dignity of the braves to aid in this. But it was considered an honour to carry a trophy of the hunt.

The herds of buffaloes were even then becoming smaller, and care was exercised that the animals should not be ruthlessly slaughtered. The Indians were as eager as the United States officials to protect the game; but the Indian police, who were charged with the enforcement of the rude game laws, were not always ready to give the red men credit for sympathetic co-operation. When Hakadah was six the comfortable buffalo-skin tepee of the family was destroyed by the police, in retaliation for a supposed Indian raid on a large herd of buffaloes. The punishment was, however, undeserved, for the lone hunter who stampeded the herd had been out after deer when he accidentally startled the heavier game. Hakadah thought the end of the world had come when the police swooped down on the camp and destroyed his home.

There were days, however, when there was neither dread of the police nor threatened raid by the Ojibways or other hostile tribes. Then Hakadah and his playmates gave themselves up to their sports. They coasted on sleds made of six or seven buffalo ribs, or of a strip of basswood bark four feet long and six inches wide. And when coasting palled, tops were brought out. American boys reserve tops for the early spring days, but these young Indians had other sports for spring. Their tops were made of wood, horn, or bone, and were heart-shaped. Buckskin was used for string. Sometimes they played singly, again from two to fifty boys joined forces, and marvelous were the figures through which the humming tops were forced.

One of the most curious sports, a war upon the nests of wild bees, is thus described: " We imagined ourselves about to make an attack upon the Ojibways or some tribal foe. We all painted and stole cautiously upon the nest; then, with a rush and a war whoop, sprang upon the object of our attack and endeavoured to destroy it. But it seemed that the bees were always on the alert and never entirely surprised, for they always raised quite as many scalps as did their bold assailants. After the onslaught on the nest was ended, we usually followed it by a pretended scalp dance. On one occasion Little Wound jumped on the fallen nest, and was immediately fiercely attacked. Relief came only when he dived into the lake near by. When he came out he was not permitted to join in the scalp dance, for he had been killed by the enemy, the Bee tribe! He did not even have the satisfaction of feeling that he had died bravely; the memory of his screams when the stings of the enraged bees surprised him was even more painful than the wounds on his face."

A popular sport was the imitation of the diversions and employments of the warriors. They built miniature tepees, they hunted, they tracked enemies through the forest. But the favourite imitation, perhaps because it was forbidden as irreverent, was the dance of the medicine men. In secret the boys would gather and go through the intricate and varied steps of the dance, until discovered by their parents and punished for their daring.

Then there was no solace but to play white man. The boys knew little of the white man. But they had heard that he laid aside the blanket by day and wore coat, hat and trousers instead; they understood, too, that he had short hair on his head and long hair on his face. And they had been told that he was always buying or selling. Several of the boys painted themselves with white clay; they wore hats of birch bark; fur provided beards; white birch bark made good shirts. Then, with sand for sugar, wild beans for coffee, dried leaves for tea, pulverized earth for gunpowder, and pebbles for bullets, they proceeded to trade with one another for the skins of wild animals.

When they tired of the land, the boys took to the water. They swam, they paddled, they used the precarious buffalo-skin boats. They also rode logs in the rapidly-flowing streams.

Of course they fished. What genuine boy can pass a stream without longing to lure, it may be trout, it may be only sunfish, from their shady retreat? Hakadah and his brothers were not different from other boys. With a hook attached to a line of horsehair or hemp, they patiently waited for the fish to bite. Sometimes they varied their sport by spearing the fish or transfixing them with arrows. Sometimes, too, they were guilty of the unsportsmanlike trick of damming the stream and driving the fish into baskets.

But training for the future warrior's life was not neglected. Hakadah listened to the legends of the tribe, and learned to repeat them. Thus he was taught to admire brave deeds and to scorn cowardly actions. When he walked in the forest he was shown how to read the story of passing animals and men, as told by fallen leaf and broken twig, by disarranged undergrowth and trampled soil; and also how to so cover his own steps that no keen-eyed enemy should observe them. He fasted on set days, and so learned endurance. Frequently the war whoop was sounded during his sleep, and he was expected to leap from his blankets to his arms. Sometimes he was sent into the depths of the forest for water on a dark night, when savage beasts and unknown enemies were about. And at all times he learned to respect those older than himself, to be silent in their presence, and to listen for their words of wisdom.

When Hakadah was twelve years old there was an unusually cold winter. A heavy fall of snow made buffalo hunting most difficult. It was impossible to use ponies in pursuing them, so dogs were employed. Preparations for this unusual expedition included the making of sleds of buffalo ribs and hickory saplings. The runners were bound with rawhide, the hair side being placed down in order that the runners might slip smoothly over the crust. On these sleds small men rode to within striking distance of a herd of buffalo. In all their movements they obeyed the orders of leaders appointed for the purpose.

The buffalo, too, had their leader, and they did their best to follow him over the snow. But progress was difficult. The animals broke through continually, and the Indians, armed with bows and arrows, or with guns, had little difficulty in coming within striking distance.

Once a buffalo fell. Wamedee jumped on his back, intending to strike the animal with his knife. But the frightened buffalo struggled to his feet, the knife was dropped and Wamedee was terrified. He implored his comrades to shoot, then begged them not to shoot, as they might kill him. He was the picture of terror. Finally the beast fell, and he scrambled to a place of safety. Always, after this experience, he was known as a coward.

Long before this Hakadah's childish name had given way to Ohiyesa (Winner). After a midsummer festival, when he had run a race in a wonderful manner, Chankpuyuhah, the medicine man, bestowed the new title upon him. How proud he was!

When Ohiyesa was fifteen he had a great surprise. His father, who had been given up for dead since the Minnesota massacre of 1863, appeared at the camp of his brother, where Ohiyesa had been living. He had learned many things about the white man's civilization, and was eager that his son should secure an education. He said:

"I am glad that my son is strong and brave. Your brothers have adopted the white man's way; I came for you to learn this way, too; and I want you to grow up a good man."

Then he urged Ohiyesa to put on the civilized clothes he had brought with him. The boy rebelled at first; he had been accustomed to hate white men and everything that belonged to them, for he had always believed that to them he owed the loss of his father. But when he reflected that they had done him no harm, after all, he thought he would try on the curious garments.

Together father and son traveled toward the haunts of the white man. As they traveled Ohiyesa listened to tales of the wonderful inventions he would see. He was especially eager to look on a railroad train. Sooner than he expected he came on the "fire-boat-walk-on-mountains." He was watering the ponies when "a peculiar shrilling noise pealed forth from just beyond the hills. The ponies threw back their heads and listened; then they ran snorting over the prairie." Ohiyesa, too, was alarmed. He leaped on the back of one of the ponies, and darted off at full speed.

The next revelation came when his father read from his Bible and talked to him about Jesus. He asked who Jesus might be. When his father explained, and told him that it was the knowledge of Jesus that had made him eager to seek his son, he was deeply impressed.

Ohiyesa was reluctant to enter on his training, until his father suggested that he make believe he was starting on a long warpath, from which there could be no honourable return until his course was completed. Entering into the spirit of the proposal, the Indian lad began his schooling at Flandreau Indian Agency and persevered through twelve years.

In 1887 he graduated from Dartmouth College. In 1890 he won his diploma at Boston University.

After leaving school he devoted himself to his people. In 1903 the government assigned to him the task of renaming the Sioux Indians. Instead of their picturesque tribal names, they were to receive English names and surnames. The story of the accomplishment of this delicate task is full of interest; his knowledge of his people and his sympathy with them enabled him to preserve the poetry of their names, while at the same time he carried out the government's purpose to bring them in touch with the white man's civilization.

VI

The Man Who " Let George Do It "

How George Westinghouse Conquered

HE let George do it. He believed in " luck."
He had a fashion of getting inspiration
from " hunches." He was always looking
for things to " break his way." Contrary to all
the teachings as to the way to succeed in life
you say? Not a bit of it. For this man succeeded
gloriously.

How did it happen? It didn't happen. Success
just had to come. He made it come.

He had a right to expect things to break his way
because he was always taking intelligent steps to
make them break in his direction.

He was inspired by his " hunches " because he
lived a sane, normal, industrious, wide-awake life,
and " hunches " simply had to come.

He was what is called a " lucky fellow," because
he lived where the only luck worth while lives—on
Hardscrabble Hill, just where Struggle Turnpike
climbs up from the Slough of Despond.

He let George do it, if George could do it better
than anybody else—because George was his name.

George Westinghouse!

The man who lighted the Chicago World's Fair!

The man whose air springs helped to make motor travel pleasanter!

The man whose compressed air brake solved many difficult problems of railroading!

Read the fascinating story of his life of achievement, as told by Francis E. Leupp, and see how everything said was true, and more.

For instance, there was the day when he, a young man, was returning from a business trip. An accident delayed the train. For two hours he watched the straining efforts of the wrecking crew to put back on the track two derailed cars.

"That was a poorly handled job," was his comment to a friend. "It was tedious," the friend replied, "but that couldn't be helped."

"Yes, it could. They could have done the whole thing in fifteen minutes by clamping a pair of rails to the track, and running them at an angle like a frog, so as to come up even against the wheels of the nearest derailed car. Then, by hitching an engine to the car, they could have shunted it back into place. In fact, it wouldn't be a bad idea for a railroad company to put together a car replacer on that principle, and have it on hand for use in emergencies."

"Why don't you make one?"

"I'll do it."

And he did—he let George do it.

In that incredibly successful sequel there was

luck, hunch, the breaking of things his way, too, if you will. But back of all was quick recognition of opportunity, readiness to decide at once, and purpose to achieve something worth while.

Take another incident.

Once more Westinghouse was on a business trip. As before, he was delayed by a wreck that his constructive mind said ought to have been avoided and might have been avoided. He said as much to a bystander who explained that, though the engineers of the wrecked trains had seen one another when yet a long way apart, they could not stop the trains in season because of the antiquated, rudimentary, impracticable chain brakes with which each car was equipped.

The words of the bystander, "The brakes wouldn't work; you can't stop a train in a moment," made him see that a brake was needed that would bring a heavy train to a stop within a few rods. Who would contrive such a brake? Let George do it!

He tried several plans, and failed. He did not know what to do next. The problem was solved by what many people would call pure luck. And it was luck—the luck of the only sort worth anything, luck that comes to anyone and everyone whose heart is set on filling his place in the world as best he can.

At noon one day a young woman entered the factory where he was at work and asked him to subscribe for *Littell's Living Age*. He felt that he had no time for reading such a periodical, and he was sending her away when her forlorn appearance made him reach for the sample magazine she carried. While turning the pages, he noted the article, " In the Mount Cenis Tunnel." Attracted, he ordered the magazine on condition that his subscription began with that number.

Examination of the article showed that it was an account of the vain efforts of the tunnel engineers to devise a plan for the work required of them in an excavation where the conditions were so unusual that no accepted methods could succeed. Their problems were solved when they made " a perforating machine, moved by common air compressed to one-sixth its natural bulk, and consequently, when set free, exercising an expansive force equal to six atmospheres."

" Eureka! " was the triumphant thought of the young inventor. " If compressed air could be conveyed through three thousand feet of pipe and yet retain enough efficiency to drive a drill through the solid stone heart of a mountain chain, it could certainly be carried the length of a railroad train and still exert the force required to set the brakes on the hindmost car."

Pure luck, wasn't it? He had a hunch! Again he let George do it, and the compressed air brake, now used all over the world, was born.

When the air brake was ready for its first public

test, there was an accident. The train had not been
out of the station more than a moment when the
driver of a frisky team was thrown across the
track, not many rods ahead of the oncoming
engine. But the engineer threw on the brakes with
all his power, and the train halted within four feet
of the prostrate man.

Pure and unadulterated luck? Yes, the sort of
luck that comes to a man who has forethought like
that which led Westinghouse to give the engineer
such careful training that he was not rattled in
time of emergency, but could coolly handle the
situation.

Just one more incident. Not long before the
Chicago World's Fair, which Westinghouse pro-
posed to light by means of his new invention, the
" stopper lamp," he was in New York when he
learned that a certain lawyer was in Pittsburgh.
Why should he think twice about the information?
To many a man it would have meant nothing. But
Westinghouse's thought ran something like this:

" I have succeeded in securing a contract to light
the World's Fair. To do so I had to underbid
Edison. At once he let me know that I could not
use his incandescent light. So I contrived a new
lamp. It is business to keep me from using this
lamp. The best way to stop me is by injunction.
The injunction would have to be secured by a lawyer, in Pittsburgh, and one of the Edison lawyers
is in Pittsburgh."

It was enough. A colleague in Pittsburgh was called by telephone, and next morning when the injunction was asked a representative of the Westinghouse interests was on hand to block the game.

What was responsible in this case? Pure hunch, wasn't it? Yes, if by hunch is meant the ability to reason things out carefully and accurately and meet situations promptly and adequately.

What does all this have to do with you? Everything, if you are fond of leaving things to George, if you sigh for a little bit of luck, if you find yourself wishing for things to break your way.

The only sure way is to make things break your way, by taking proper measures to that end; to be prepared for whatever comes.

It is safe to let George do it—provided *you* are George. But you must be persistent, and you must be patient.

VII

The Cadmus of the Blind

What Samuel Gridley Howe Accomplished

THOSE who knew Samuel Gridley Howe as a boy thought of him as anything but "the born philanthropist" he was later called by his friend and biographer, F. B. Sanborn. He was so fond of pranks that when, years after his graduation from Brown University, he returned for a brief call on the president, who had known him for four years, he was received with a look of alarm. The president motioned him to a chair, "took his own seat at a distance and kept a wary eye on his former pupil." The visitor began to apologize for the pranks for which he had been distinguished at college, but the good president interrupted him. "I declare, Howe," he cried, moving his chair still farther back, "I am afraid of you now! I'm afraid there will be a torpedo under my chair before I know it."

The memory of those college pranks gave Dr. Howe keen regret as he looked back on them, but his children liked to hear him describe them. It is his daughter, Laura E. Richards, who writes of them thus:

"When the president's horse was led up to the

very top of one of the college buildings and left there overnight, or when ink was squirted through a keyhole at a too curious tutor whose eye happened to be on the other side, the authorities only felt that here was a naughty lad who was getting himself and others into trouble, and bringing discredit upon the college, and Sam Howe was rusticated once and again."

Dr. Howe's eye would twinkle as he " told how funny the old horse looked, stretching his meek head out of the fourth-story window and whinnying mournfully to his amazed master below." But he did not fail to tell those who listened to him that if he could live his college days over he would not be guilty of such pranks. It was his regret that he did not realize in time what it meant to his father to send one of his boys to college. The father had once been in comfortable circumstances, but after the War of 1812, when he had furnished the government a large quantity of rope and cordage of his own manufacture for which he was never paid, he was compelled to reduce expenses.

However, he decided that he could manage to pay the bills of one of his three sons at college. But which should it be? His method of deciding among the three was characteristic of the man, his biographer writes. " Calling them up before him he opened the big family Bible, and bade each in turn read a chapter aloud. ' The one who reads best,' he said, ' shall go to college.' Probably there was little doubt as to the choice, for my father was always an admirable reader; at all events, it fell upon him. Joseph went into business, Edward to sea, while Samuel entered Brown University, in 1818, in the seventeenth year of his age."

When he entered college he was a mere stripling, but he was so well built, so attractive in every way, that every stranger who passed him turned to look at him. What impressed his companions most, was his quickness in emergencies. "Before anybody else had time to think, his plan was formed," a classmate said of him.

This quickness was characteristic from the day when, as a boy of nine or ten, he rescued himself from the Back Bay while enjoying the sport of jumping from cake to cake of floating ice, to the years of sedate manhood when the cares of life came thick and fast. Two instances are related by his daughter. Once, soon after his marriage to Julia Ward—whose name will always be remembered so long as the " Battle Hymn of the Republic " is sung—he was traveling with her by carriage in Italy. Dr. Howe had stepped into an inn to make an inquiry, leaving the carriage in charge of the driver. The driver left his seat for a moment. While he was gone the horses ran away with Mrs. Howe, the nurse and the baby. Dr. Howe came running out and pursued the flying horses. " Rounding a corner, he saw at a little distance a country wagon coming slowly toward him, drawn by a stout horse, the wagoner half asleep on the seat. My father ran up, stopped the horse, cut the traces, leaped on his back, and was off before the astonished driver could utter a word." The runaways were quickly overtaken. Then the countryman was liberally rewarded for the use of his horse.

The second incident occurred when Dr. Howe was at the head of the Perkins Institute for the Blind. He was seated with his family at dinner in the house near by when a breathless messenger ran into the dining-room gasping out the tidings that the institute was on fire. Between the house and the institution was a great hill, sloping from the garden wall, and terminating on the side toward the institution in an abrupt precipice some sixty feet high. The bearer of the bad news had been forced to come around through several streets, thus losing precious minutes; but the doctor did not know what it was to lose a minute. Before anyone could speak or ask what he would do, he was out of the house, ran through the garden, climbed the slope at the back, rushed like a flame across the green hilltop, and slid down the almost vertical face of the precipice. Bruised and panting he reached the institution, and saw at a glance that the fire was in the upper story. Take time to go round to the door and up the stairs? Not he! He " swarmed up " the gutter spout, and in less time than it takes to tell it was on the roof, cutting away the burning

timbers with an ax which he had got hold of, no
one knew how.

At the end of his college course, Sam Howe realized that it was high time to give serious thought
to the question how to fill a man's place in the
world. He decided to take a medical course, probably planning to begin the practice of his profession
in Boston. But this was not to be. His attention
was drawn to the brave struggle of the Greeks to
throw off the yoke of their Turkish oppressors.
They needed help. Why, then, should not he offer
his services? He could serve as a surgeon, binding
up the wounds of the patriotic men who were falling for their country.

When he spoke of his plans to his father there
was bitter opposition, but Dr. Howe's motto all
through life was, " Obstacles are things to be overcome," so he was not daunted. In the end his
father gave him money toward his expenses, and
in 1824 the young man sailed for Greece.

Then followed several years when he marched
with the Greeks, sharing their hardships and becoming their hero. In later life he was ready to
talk of the bravery of his comrades, but of his own
conspicuous part in their campaigns he was not
anxious to say much. " He was inclined never to
talk about himself; his own exploits interested him
far less than those of anyone else; but speaking of
those days once, he said: ' I knew more than once
what you probably never had any realizing sense

of, to wit, the sharp gnawings of real hunger. You know only what a good appetite is; you do not know what a ravening vulture it becomes when it grows bad. I have been months without eating other flesh than mountain snails or roasted wasps; weeks without bread and days without a morsel of food of any kind. Woe to the stray donkey or goat that fed within our reach then; they were quickly slain, and their flesh, cut up hastily in little square bits, was roasting on our ramrods or devoured half raw.' "

Events proved that the brave Greeks had undertaken too large a contract. Years of war brought extreme poverty to the land. Thousands were dying of hunger and of the plagues that accompany hunger. Then Dr. Howe responded to the appeal of Greece and went to America to plead her cause and to secure funds for relief. He told how the Greeks would be overcome by absolute starvation, in spite of the determination to hold out. " All the able-bodied men of the nation were in the field. The Turks had devastated the land, and there were no hands to till it."

The funds received by Dr. Howe in response to this plea were distributed by him in a statesman-like manner. He had seen the evil of indiscriminate giving when no return was asked, so he made known his purpose to give food and clothing to all in need, provided those who were able would work for it. His method was illustrated at Ægina, where the harbour was in a miserable state of repair. It was necessary to build a wall a few feet from the shore line. Stones for this must be brought and the space between the wall and the shore filled with broken stone. Not far away were the ruins of the ancient temple of Venus. There was his chance! Hundreds of labourers were set to work excavating stone from the ruins and transporting it to the shore, while skilled workmen were told to build the wall. When this was done there was rubbish in plenty to fill the space. Thus the harbour was prepared anew, hundreds of people were saved from starvation, and by their own efforts, and the city was left in a better position to care for itself thereafter.

Of course, friends at home criticised the doctor, but he was not disturbed. To his father he wrote: " You say this will not raise me in the opinion of the sensible part of the community. I care not. My friends, those who know my motives, will better appreciate my services; my reward will be in that."

He remained in Greece until the patriots were aided by the diplomacy of the powers of western Europe to recover a place among the nations.

In 1831, when Dr. Howe returned to America, the trustees appointed by the Massachusetts Legislature to open an Asylum for the Blind, the first of its kind in America, were trying to decide on a man to lead in the enterprise. The proposition was made to Dr. Howe. With his usual quick decision he grasped the opportunity, and so began his life work.

Within a few days he was on his way to Europe, where he visited institutions for the education of the blind. Enthusiasm grew as he saw the great need and the marvelous results. He could scarcely wait for the time of his return, he was so eager to begin his work.

In America once more, he scoured the country for blind children, brought them together as the nucleus of the institution, devised methods for their instruction, breaking the way as truly as his pioneer ancestors had done when they cleared the forest, for there were no precedents. His enthusiasm was contagious. The legislature gave liberally for the work, the public became interested. By the assistance of the American Bible Society the Bible was prepared for the blind at an expenditure of thirteen thousand dollars, and other books were added to the library of the Perkins Institution, which now contains nearly two thousand volumes in raised print. The printing of these volumes was made possible by his own improvement on the French system of writing for the blind.

The success of the work in Massachusetts attracted the attention of the entire country. Calls for Dr. Howe's presence in other cities were frequent. In response to these calls the busy man went to seventeen different state legislatures, urging them to provide for the education of the blind. In many instances he was successful.

Dr. Howe was especially interested in children who were deaf and dumb as well as blind. Wherever he went he turned aside to see them. He found several in England when he was on his wedding tour. Others were discovered on the continent of Europe. " In every case he did all that he could to awaken interest in them and to insure their instruction. Whenever it was possible he gave the instruction himself, giving several lessons in the presence of some person who, he hoped, would be moved to continue the work."

Sometimes he was able to keep the unfortunate children under his own eye. This was so in the case of Laura Bridgman, with whom he did his greatest individual work. Laura was deaf, dumb, blind, without the sense of smell and with imperfect taste. In 1837 she was brought to the institution. Dr. Howe devoted himself to her instruction. The story of how he brought her out of darkness into light is one of the wonder tales of American scientific achievements. She became a member of his household; his daughter, Laura E. Richards, was named for her.

But great as were Dr. Howe's labours for the blind, it must not be thought that his efforts were limited to them. His heart was very tender toward all who were unfortunate. He lived in accordance with his word to others:

" There floats not in the stream of life any wreck of humanity so shattered and crippled that its signals of distress should not challenge attention and command assistance."

As a member of the legislature, he assisted Miss Dorothea Dix in pushing through her bill for the correction of the inhuman prison system of the state and the proper care of the insane who were herded with criminals. His work for the correction of educational methods in Boston was characterized by one man as "one which only Sam Howe or an angel could have done." Observing that nothing had been done for the idiotic and the feeble-minded, he aroused the state and was instrumental in securing a school for their care and training. He was a leader in anti-slavery work, and, later in life, he was a chosen adviser of presidents and an envoy sent abroad in cases of importance. As a member of the Board of Charities he continued to mold the state's charitable system until it became a model. So the busy years were passed until, at seventy-five years of age, he answered God's call to lay his armor down and went into the presence of Him in whose name he had cared for the suffering.

Of the many messages spoken in eulogy of Dr. Howe this, written by Governor Bullock, of Massachusetts, was one of the most striking:

" Over the tomb of this philanthropist, I would not hang out his insignia of the Greek Legion of

Honour, nor his Cross of Malta, nor his medal of Prussia. I would instead record the words of Edmund Burke applied by him to John Howard and his mission: 'He penetrated into the depths of dungeons; he plunged into the infections of hospitals; he surveyed the mansions of sorrow and pain; he took the gauge and dimensions of misery, depression and contempt; he remembered the forgotten; he attended to the neglected, he visited the forsaken and he compared and collated the distresses of all men in all countries.' "

Edward Everett Hale wrote:

" You ask for his epitaph. It is a very simple epitaph. He found idiots chattering, taunted and ridiculed by each village fool, and he left them cheerful and happy. He found the insane shut up in their wretched cells, miserable, starving, cold and dying, and he left them happy, hopeful and brave. He found the blind sitting in darkness, and he left them glad in the sunshine of the love of God."

VIII

The Way of a Sailing Ship

The Hard Discipline That Made Richard Henry Dana, Jr.

"A LONG, low, dark room, with wooden benches well cut up, walls nearly black, and a close hot atmosphere."

This was the description of the schoolroom in Cambridgeport, Massachusetts, in which Richard Henry Dana, Jr., began his education. Though he was then but eight years old, the school made such an impression on him that many years later he wrote concerning it:

"When the time came for dismissing school, the books were put away, the names of all the delinquents called over, the closet unlocked, and the long pine ferule produced. How often did our hearts sicken at the sight of that closet and that ferule! The boys were then called out, one at a time, and the blows given upon the flat of their hands, from two to four up to one or two dozen, according to the nature of the offense and the size of the boy. A few of the older boys never cried, but only changed color violently as the blows fell; but the other boys always cried and some lustily and with good reason."

Oliver Wendell Holmes added his reminiscences of that early school. He said he remembered Dana "as a little rosy-faced, sturdy boy, piloting an atom of a younger brother, Edmund, to and from the schoolroom." He also recalled a brutal punishment described as "dragging the boys about by their ears across the school-room and over the benches." He said that Dana was once the victim of this brutal method of punishment. One of the older boys made Dana laugh. When he kept on laughing, his ear was pulled. Unable to control himself, he laughed still more. Then he was dragged by the ear to his seat. The older pupil continued the antics that provoked the laughter. Dana enraged the master still more. He seized the boy by the ear and dragged him over the back of his seat. As a result the ear was badly injured, and this method of punishment was forbidden by the school committee.

A change was made some time later to the private school taught by Ralph Waldo Emerson, then a young college graduate. In 1842 Dana spoke of him as a very pleasant instructor, "although he had not system or discipline enough to insure regular and vigorous study."

There was no lack of system and discipline in a later school where the master, a man whom Dana called "Mr. W.," for some slight breach of discipline, inflicted a punishment that aroused great indignation, even in that day when severe corporal

punishment in the school was considered a necessity. It is possible to tell of this punishment in the
words of the victim, as these were recorded many
years later:

" He ordered me to put out my left hand. Upon
this hand he inflicted six blows with all his
strength, and then six upon the right hand. I was
in such a frenzy of indignation at his injustice
. . . that I could not have uttered a word for my
life. I was too small and slender to resist, and
could show my spirit only by fortitude. He called
for my right hand again, and gave six more blows
in the same manner, and then six more upon the
left. My hands were swollen and in acute pain,
but I did not flinch nor show a sign of suffering.
He was determined to conquer and gave six more
blows upon each hand, with full force. Still there
was no sign from me of pain or submission. I
could have gone to the stake for what I considered
my honour. The school was in an uproar of hiss-
ing and scraping and groaning, and the master
turned his attention to the other boys and let me
alone. . . . I went in the afternoon to the trustees
of the school, stated my case, produced my evi-
dence, and had an examination made. The next
morning but four boys went to school, and the day
following the career of Mr. W. ended."

Dana's recollections, as quoted by his biographer,
Charles Francis Adams, give still another valuable
glimpse of the schools of the day. When he was

fifteen years old he attended a Cambridge boarding and day school, where his preparation for college was to be completed. Of this establishment, which was attended by about thirty boys, he said:

" All but about half a dozen were boarders, and either sons of men of property in Boston, or of Southern gentlemen. The accommodations for the boys were as follows: four large rooms in the attic. in which they slept, six or seven in a room, and to which they were not permitted to go except for sleeping, or for some special purpose, upon leave. There were no fires in these rooms, and I believe but one light in the entry for all the rooms. . . . At all events the boys were never allowed a light except for a few minutes, to go to bed with. There was a wash-room, also without a fire, with half a dozen tin basins and towels, for the boys' washing. There was a dining-room, reserved for meals, and never entered for any other purpose. The school-room was the only room in which the boys could be, except when in bed, by day or night, and in which they must do all their reading, writing, thinking, conversing, and in which their characters and habits were formed. This room was oblong, rather small for the number of boys it was to accommodate, with a stove in the middle, and but one light in the evening for all the boys, and that a lamp fastened to the wall higher than the boys' heads, and of such a kind and so placed that but two or three boys could read by it at the same time.

Indeed, what with the noise of so many boys in one room, the necessity of going away from the stove, and the poor accommodations under this lamp, very little reading was done. Those boys who passed several years at this school before entering college went to college the most ignorant young men upon all subjects of literature and of that knowledge acquired through books, and the society of educated persons."

This sounds more like the description of a military prison than of a school of academic grade. And the unfavourable impression is intensified by further particulars: " There were bounds beyond which the scholars were never permitted to go. These bounds included the yard about the house and the playground adjoining; but none of the favourite games of foot-ball, hand-ball, base or cricket, could be played in the grounds with any satisfaction, for the ball would be constantly flying over the fence, beyond which the boys could not go without asking special leave. This was a damper upon the more ranging and athletic exercises. Flying kite, too, was of course out of the question, as that requires a long run to raise the kite and sometimes a chase after it, if the string should break."

Here, too, corporal punishment was an every-day affair. " The master always had a rattan either in hand or lying on his desk; and if any disorder was observed, or a boy had not his lesson prepared, the master sprang up, and down went the rattan upon

the boy's back. There were about half a dozen
boys who were flogged regularly every day, and
who detested the sight of school-room, master and
books. There was never a half-day without a good
deal of flogging."

In spite of the shortcomings of the masters who
taught him, Dana was able to enter college at sixteen. At once he took high rank in his class. But
his career was interrupted toward the end of
Freshman year when he was " rusticated," along
with many of his classmates, because of their ideas
of honour in standing by a charity student, who
refused to inform on a fellow who had broken
the rules. The six months of this rustication he
spent with a young minister who later became
President of Bowdoin College. The close association with him required by the terms of his sus-
pension counted for a great deal in Dana's development, for the temporary schoolmaster was a man
of unusual attainments and ability to impart knowledge and to inspire to manly living.

A second interruption in the course came at the
beginning of Junior year. An attack of measles
left the student with impaired eyesight. For a time
he could not endure the light. For several months
he tried to maintain his place in class, but all efforts
to read were painful. At last, reluctantly, he left
college.

The biographer says that many a young man of
eighteen would have given up in despair, thinking

it useless to try to make anything of himself. But Dana was made of sterner stuff. He tried to think of some method by which he might regain his ability to study. He knew that it was out of the question to go to Europe, as the son of a wealthy man would have done in his circumstances. Yet he felt that travel was the one hopeful remedy for his ailment. Thinking that the time had come when he could properly satisfy his hunger for adventure, he proposed a long sea trip. When his wishes were known, he received a number of offers to go as cabin passenger in one of the first clipper ships bound for India. But he knew that he needed a rougher experience than this, " so he made up his mind to go before the mast, wisely reasoning that hard work, plain diet, and open-air life would by effecting a gradual change in his whole physical system gradually restore his eyesight."

Though his father felt that the program eagerly outlined to him was impractical, he finally agreed to let his son do as he thought best, and on the day before his nineteenth birthday he sailed from Boston for California.

During his absence from home of more than two years he kept a journal which he afterward developed into the book, " Two Years Before the Mast," which has been read by hundreds of thousands of boys and has long been considered a classic tale of sea-life.

This is the way he began the story:

" 'The fourteenth of August was the day fixed upon for the sailing of the brig Pilgrim, on her voyage from Boston, round Cape Horn, to the western coast of North America. As she was to get under way early in the afternoon, I made my appearance on board at twelve o'clock, in full sea-rig, with my chest, containing an outfit for a two or three years' voyage.

" The change from the tight frock coat, silk cap, and kid gloves of an undergraduate at Harvard, to the loose duck trousers, checked shirt, and tarpaulin hat of a sailor, though somewhat of a transformation, was soon made, and I supposed that I should pass very well for a jack tar. But it is impossible to deceive the practised eye in these matters; and while I thought myself to be looking as salt as Neptune himself, I was, no doubt known for a landsman by every one on board as soon as I hove in sight. A sailor has a peculiar cut to his clothes, and a way of wearing them which a green hand can never get. The trousers, tight round the hips, and thence hanging long and loose around the feet, a superabundance of checked shirt, a low-crowned, well-varnished black hat, worn on the back of the head, with half a fathom of black ribbon hanging over the left eye, and a slip-tie to the black silk neckerchief, with sundry other minutiæ, are signs, the want of which betrays the beginner at once."

The story is full of movement. Something is happening all the time. Once it was the cry, " Man overboard," when a sailor who was the life of the crew fell from the starboard fettock shrouds, and not knowing how to swim, and being heavily dressed, probably sank immediately. The author was in the boat that put out for him, but all in vain.

Then there is the story of the captain who mistreated one of his men, flogging him to within an inch of his life, and the racy narrative of how the vessel's cargo of hides was taken on in the ports of California.

One of the best passages is the story of an eighty-mile race between two swift sailing vessels. First one was ahead, then another. No one knew how the race would end. "Thus we continued ahead, astern, and abreast of each other, alternately, now far out at sea, and again close in under the shore." At last the smaller vessel, which spread less canvas, came into port the winner.

Once the author, with some others, was overtaken in a storm when out in an open boat. They managed to reach the shore, where they slept on wet logs, and made a fire in a saucepan, in which they cooked mussels dug up on the beach, and in other ways showed that they were able to look out for themselves in an emergency.

The voyage resulted in decided physical benefit; it made of a weak stripling a robust man. But better even than this, it taught him self-reliance and fitted him to fight the battle of life as he could not have done without it.

His biographer calls attention to the fact that he was handicapped by his descent from prominent ancestors. "His chances for achieving distinction would have been incomparably better had he been the son of some Congregational clergyman settled in a poor country parish; for in America it is not well for any young man to grow up under the consciousness of an ancestry or incumbered by family traditions. Dana not only did so grow up, but he was naturally disposed to dwell upon this sort of thing and to magnify its importance. . . . The forecastle experience arrested morbid action, or, in homely language, took the nonsense out of him. He could no longer be a dreamer, in danger of becoming a little later on what is sometimes called a 'prig,' and turned out a tough, manly, sensible young fellow, afraid of nothing, eager to please and succeed, resolute, unselfish and honest. . . . That which would have ruined a coarser nature simply toned him up to the proper level. He ceased to be too fine for every-day use. Indeed, all through his subsequent life a sort of conflict may be observed between the saving inspiration of the forecastle and hereditary instincts and traditions. In the prime of his manhood the first predominated and led to an early and brilliant career; as the years went on the freshness of the great lesson faded away, and influences which antedated his birth and surrounded his life asserted themselves, not for his good."

Six months' study enabled him to graduate with the Harvard Class of 1837. He had been quickened mentally as well as physically because, as Mr. Adams says, " his mind had been lying fallow." That he was at this time sensitive to spiritual impressions as well was evident when, soon after his graduation, he became a Christian and united with the Episcopal Church, of which he continued an active member to the end of his days.

Following his graduation from college came several years in the Dane Law School, where he distinguished himself by careful work. At the same time he was instructor in elocution at Harvard. The double employment kept him busy, but not too busy to write out the manuscript of " Two Years Before the Mast."

It was his hope that the book would be sufficiently remunerative to enable him to marry; he had no funds, and he knew he was dependent on his own efforts. William Cullen Bryant, who read the manuscript, thought it well worth printing. He took it to publishers in New York who submitted it to one of their best readers. His advice was that the firm should purchase it " at any price necessary to secure it." The publishers offered to buy the book, but refused to consider the paying of a royalty. When terms were under discussion, Mr. Bryant suggested five hundred dollars, but the best the publishers would agree to was two hundred and fifty dollars. And for this ridiculous price the classic was finally sold.

From the first sales were large, so that the publishers reaped a reward out of all proportion to their investment.

It is pleasant to record the fact that a London publisher, impressed by the book, brought out an edition as soon as possible, and paid the author a larger sum than he had received from his American publishers. They were under no legal obligation to do this, as there was no international copyright. But their sense of right led them to do what proved very profitable to them, for the book from the first has been popular in England.

The author did not realize the extent of the sales there till he made his first visit to England, in 1856; then he found that the way had been paved for him by the volume which has been pointed out as a model both in matter and style.

The experience that led to the writing of the book had much to do with determining the manner of Dana's law practice. His knowledge of ships made him a favourite advocate in nautical cases. His sympathy with the men before the mast, who were so often abused, was responsible for his taking their part in many an unprofitable case. This readiness to fight for the under-dog led him to undertake a number of cases of negroes who were seized in Massachusetts, under the Fugitive Slave law. Perhaps it had something to do with the prominent part he took in the organization of the Free Soil party.

Many disappointments came to him during the latter part of his forty years' service of his fellows, but always his faith in God enabled him to forget hard things.

When, on January 6, 1882, he died in Rome, Italy, his wife chose for his last resting place the old Protestant cemetery in the Eternal City.

IX

The Millionaire Who Chose to Die Poor

How Daniel K. Pearsons Gave Away His Fortune

"HE had no childhood!" was once said pityingly of Daniel Kimball Pearsons, who was born April 14, 1820, on a farm several miles from Bradford, Vermont. The remark was made because John Pearsons, the father, had a large family to support on a meager income, and it was therefore necessary for the sons to do what they could to make their own way, even when quite young.

But the subject of the pitying remarks always denied their truth. He insisted that the necessity of doing hard work did not keep him from having a good time. When he skated on the Connecticut River or coasted on Potato Hill or joined with his companions in playing town ball, he enjoyed himself all the more because of the hours devoted to work; these gave zest to the hours he could give to sport.

While his parents were able to provide nothing for the financial future of their children, they gave what was far more worth while, training in a Christian home, the heritage of an honoured name and inspiration for self-sacrificing service of others. On Sunday the family walked to Bradford for church and Sunday school, and during the week the children were witnesses of the earnest life of their parents that was in keeping with the Sabbath teachings in the village church. " He was the honestest man I ever knew," was the testimony Daniel later gave concerning his father, and his words concerning his mother's Christian character were just as enthusiastic.

During the summer, and on Saturdays and at odd hours during the winter, Daniel helped his father on the farm. At ten he was a thorough-going little farmer; his knowledge of agriculture was greater than his years would indicate, while the amount of work done was far greater than that accomplished by the average ten-year-old boy.

After spending a number of winters at the district school he told his parents of his desire for an education that would fit him to fill a larger place in the world. They were sympathetic, but could give him little more than good advice. So, with their blessing, he went to the Bradford Academy and later to the Montpelier Conference (now Newbury) Seminary. Here he lived on forty cents a week in addition to the aid, chiefly provisions, which he received from home. During the term he earned by odd jobs the necessary money to pay for tuition, books and clothing. In telling of these experiences, and of later experiences at college, he once said : " For five years I boarded myself, baked my own johnnycake, cooked my own potatoes, fried my own meat. For five years I depended upon myself entirely and during that time I waxed fat in the doing of it, and was well and hearty at all times."

In later years the memory of this experience made him unwilling to advance money to students to pay college expenses. " It doesn't pay to help young men through college that way," he would say. " I have tried it dozens of times. . . . It is little to me, but it is bad for them. It is a calamity. It destroys the initiative. The boy or girl who is determined to get through college cannot be restrained by any difficulty. Such people will 'work their way through untold hardships."

Montpelier Seminary always had a warm place in his heart. There he had one teacher whose influence on his life was very great, and there he began his Christian life.

From the seminary he went to Dartmouth College, where he succeeded in paying his expenses for a year, his board costing him less than a dollar a week.

When he was sixteen years old he applied for a school. For several years he was a teacher. Then he went to Boston to seek a clerkship in a store. He tramped the streets for days in search of a situation, but without success. When his money was nearly gone, he applied to a farmer at Faneuil

Hall market, and was taken to the man's dairy farm at Brookline. There, for four months, he worked for fifteen dollars a month and board. Then he followed his employer's advice and entered a manual-training school.

Toward the end of the year a committee in search of a teacher applied to the school for a student. After examining several young men without success, they inquired for "the young man from Vermont, who had paid his way by his work." Young Pearsons was engaged, and taught with great satisfaction to everyone.

While in charge of the school at Lynnfield, Massachusetts, he had an encounter with a bully who threatened to break up the school. The bully was soundly thrashed. A lawsuit followed, the teacher being charged with assault and battery. The teacher was acquitted, the judge declaring that "the young man had made the assault and the teacher had applied the battery."

At twenty-one years of age the ambitious young Vermonter entered the medical school at Woodstock. After receiving his diploma he practiced medicine at Chicopee, Massachusetts.

Before long he became a visitor at the home of Deacon Chapin, where he met two women who were to have a great influence on his life. One of these was Marietta Chapin, who became his wife several years later. Of her influence on him during the sixty years of their life together Dr. Pearsons said, when an old man: " Whatever I am, I owe to my wife. She interested me in everything good. To her belongs the credit of all that I have done. I trusted her judgment; I never knew it to fail. I always told her everything, and always followed her advice."

The second woman met in the Chicopee home was Mary Lyon, who was devoting her life to the cause of Mount Holyoke College. Observation of her work and talks with him about her ideals made him more than ever interested in the education of boys and girls, and he determined that if ever he were able he would give largely to such schools as hers.

Dr. Pearsons was a success as a physician, but Mrs. Pearsons told him he could make more of himself if he would go West. So he sold his practice and in 1851 went with her on a prospecting tour of which he sometimes gave this reminiscence:

" Our destination was Janesville, Wisconsin, and we passed through Elgin, which was then a terminus of the railroad. From there we took muck wagons to our destination, passing through Beloit. We passed through a good deal of mud, and it was rich mud. When we reached Beloit we had to ford the Rock River, and our horses swam the river. We had to stand up on the seats to keep our feet from getting wet. We stopped at a little tavern to rest. Beloit was a small hamlet.

" When we started on, a big burly fellow climbed

into the wagon for a ride. I noticed a brick building going up and asked him what was being done.
He answered:

" ' There are some Yankee cranks building a
college.'

" That rather interested me, for I was just out of
New England, and a thorough Yankee, and proud
of it. If anybody calls me a Yankee I take off my
hat and bow. If he calls me an ' Old Puritan,' I
make three bows.

" On the way to Janesville that man cursed
everything that was good. I tried to argue with
him and to stand up for a Christian education the
best I knew how. When we got to Janesville I
shook my fist in his face and I said, ' Young man,
I am going West and I am going to get rich, and
when I do I am coming back to lift up these colleges that Yankee cranks are founding.' "

But the self-confessed Yankee was not to go
farther West. After a brief stay in the vicinity of
Janesville, he returned East, and soon accepted a
proposition to make a trip through the southern
states to introduce textbooks on physiology in the
schools. During the course of his work he developed unsuspected capacity as a lecturer. For four
years he varied appearances before audiences with
business ventures which always succeeded.

Dr. Pearsons' success in his own schemes led a
Massachusetts owner of land in Illinois to ask him
to go West to sell the land on commission. The

land was sold with satisfaction to owner and purchaser alike. More business was given to him. He was known as a man of his word, and everyone had confidence in him. As agent for the sale of Illinois Central Railroad Company lands, he opened the way for thousands of farmers to make their homes near the line of the road.

He began to make investments for himself. In 1860 he decided he must make his home in Chicago, then a city of one hundred and twelve thousand population. The first home was in a five-dollar-a-week boarding house. His first office was desk room for which he paid twenty-five dollars a year. This was a prophecy of the simplicity that characterized his life even when he was possessed of millions.

From the city as a center he continued his trips to the farming lands of the state until his own business became so large that he had to turn over the land agency to others. Then he made investments in city real estate and in Michigan pine lands that soon brought him large wealth.

But he was not so deeply engrossed in business that he would not serve others. After the Chicago fire, when men of integrity and ability were needed by the city, he served as alderman, devoting to the office time that would have been worth to himself at least fifty thousand dollars a year. As a member of the Finance Committee of the Council he was a large factor in restraining the city from ruinous courses, thus restoring the confidence of Eastern investors. Just when the city was having greatest difficulty in meeting the demands on it, an issue of scrip, which had been sold in New York, was declared illegal by the courts. The Finance Committee refused to take advantage of the decision. Dr. Pearsons was asked by the mayor to go to New York to allay the fears of investors who were clamoring for their money. He satisfied them all. In one case he offered to pay the claims of the complainant. That offer carried the day. The man seemed to think that an investment good enough for Dr. Pearsons was good enough for him.

During these years of stress the man who was making money to give it away did not make the mistake of giving nothing while he saved. To the First Presbyterian Church, of which he was an earnest member, he gave liberally both of time and money. Churches, institutions and individuals in many places shared in his giving—or, rather in the giving of husband and wife, for he used to say that the gifts were just as much from Mrs. Pearsons as from him.

The fortune increased. "Expenses were kept at the lowest point possible, consistent with comfortable living," his biographer, Edward F. Williams, has said. "With household expenses never exceeding two or three thousand dollars a year, and personal expenses reduced to a minimum, it is not difficult to see that with an income that often averaged three thousand dollars a week, money would accumulate rapidly."

Once some young men asked him how he explained his ability to earn and save. " I'll tell you boys a secret," he said. " I did it by keeping my character clean. That's the only thing I had to start with, and it is the best thing any man can have. Without it you are not worth a picayune."

In 1889 Dr. Pearsons astonished everybody by doing what he said he would do some day; he retired from business and devoted himself to giving away the fortune which had been made for this distinct purpose. From his home in Hinsdale, Illinois, he went here and there over the country, searching for good places to invest his gifts. At first he gave to institutions of various kinds. Then he decided that his particular field should be the small denominational colleges. He gave to many institutions in many states, without regarding their denominational connection. It was his custom to offer a certain sum on condition that a much larger sum should be raised in a given time.

One of the institutions to which he gave most largely was Beloit College, thus fulfilling the prophecy of that day in the spring of 1851 when a fellow traveler on the stage made sport of the Yankee College. He gave also to Mount Holyoke, whose founder he had met when he was a young physician; to Montpelier Seminary, Vermont,

where he had struggled for an education; to Lake
Forest College, and to two score other institutions.
As a result of his gifts small colleges in many
states were given a new lease of life and are doing
work that counts heavily.

In all he gave away perhaps seven million dollars, enough to build and endow a great " Pearsons
College." But he chose rather to distribute his
gifts where they would go with the gifts of others,
and much more good be done than would be possible in any institution he could build.

In 1909 he said: " I am having more fun than
any other millionaire alive. Let other rich men go
in for automobiles and steam yachts. I have discovered, after endowing forty-seven colleges in
twenty-four different states, that giving is the most
exquisite of all mundane delights. On my ninetieth
birthday, I am going to have a squaring up with all
the small colleges I have promised money to, and I
serve notice now that I am going on a new ram-
page of giving. I intend to die penniless. If there
are any other millionaires who want to have a lot
of fun, let them follow my example."

On his ninety-first birthday he completed his giving, and was practically a poor man. At that time
he said:

" I now have finished my career as a giver. I
had a good time making my money, and I have had
a better time spending it. I am an old man now. I
have reached the limit which I set for myself. I

have paid the last dollar of my pledges, and now I propose to rest. Henceforth I will consider no more pleas. With this I retire. I lie down to-night a free man. I do not owe a dollar in the world, and I have no outstanding pledges."

He made this further statement in explanation of his hobby of giving to colleges:

" I gave to colleges because I believe in young manhood and young womanhood. I gave to poor colleges, because I believe in young people who have to struggle. I gave to Christian colleges because I believe that education without character is a very doubtful blessing."

Last of all he gave away his beautiful house, to be used by Hinsdale for a library. Then he retired to a sanitarium, where he lived very simply until his death, April 14, 1912.

Andrew Carnegie said of this princely giver that there has never been in the history of America a case of giving which accomplished so much of value to the whole country as the gifts of Dr. Pearsons to the small colleges of the West.

X

The Story of a Working Philanthropist

How George W. Childs Conquered the Hearts of Men

IT is recorded that when Charles Dickens as a boy saw the great house, Gadshill, he made up his mind that some day he would be the owner of the place. This ambition of boyhood was his inspiration through years of struggle till he was able to carry out his purpose. In like manner, George W. Childs, when a working boy, determined that one day he would own the *Public Ledger,* the Philadelphia newspaper that did more to mould public opinion in the Quaker City than all its contemporaries. And he persevered till his ambition was realized.

He was a born business man. James Parton says that when at school he was always bartering his boyish treasures, knives for pigeons, marbles for pop-guns, a bird-cage for a book.

Very early he found it necessary to leave school and go to work. His first employment was when he was twelve years old, as errand-boy in a bookstore in Baltimore, where he was born on May 12,

1829. His pay here was two dollars a week. In his Recollections, written when he was sixty years old, he said that he was always eager for work, that he enjoyed it, and that he believed he earned every cent of his first money.

When he was thirteen years old he spent fifteen months in the United States Navy. Fortunately he did not like the service and secured his discharge. After another short taste of school life, he went to Philadelphia. Of his work in a bookstore there, where he was both clerk and errand boy, he wrote:

"I would get up very early in the morning, go down to the store and wash the pavement and put things in order before breakfast, and in the winter time would make the fire and sweep out the store."

He was ready to work until late at night whenever this was necessary, desiring to give the best possible value for the three dollars he received every week. Eager to make himself more useful, he began to frequent the evening book auctions, and so became familiar with the titles and prices of books. Before long his employer entrusted to him the purchase of books at these auctions. Early the next morning after a sale the book buyer would become the errand boy; as soon as the store was opened and swept he would go after his purchases with a wheelbarrow. "I have never outgrown this habit of doing things directly and in order," he wrote. "I would to-day as lief carry a bundle up

Chestnut Street from the *Ledger* Office as I would then."

For four years the young book-buyer improved his opportunities, increasing in proficiency until his employer decided to send him every six months to New York and Boston, to attend the book sales there. Thus he became acquainted with many other book-buyers and publishers whose acquaintance proved to be of great value to him in later years.

Although his wages were always small, he was only eighteen when he decided that he could safely go into business for himself. So he set up a modest store in the old *Public Ledger* building. Then began his purpose to own not only the great newspaper, but the *Ledger* building as well. Wise management, genial manners, and skilful handling of his customers made the business a success from the first.

As he sold books, he dreamed of the day when he could publish them also. Three years passed before the way was open for taking the next step in his career. Then, at twenty-one, he became junior partner in the publishing firm of R. E. Peterson & Company, afterwards Childs & Peterson. One of the first issues of the new firm threatened to swamp them, but proved to be the making of the house. Of this book, Dr. Kane's "Arctic Explorations," Mr. Childs wrote in 1889:

"When the work was ready to be issued, I took

a sample copy to New York, to solicit orders from the leading booksellers. The largest house would give me only a small order. 'Mr. Childs,' they said, 'you won't sell more than a thousand altogether.' They ordered at first only one hundred copies, but soon after sent for five thousand more to meet the demand. Within one year after the publication we paid Dr. Kane a copyright of nearly seventy thousand dollars. It was the Doctor's original intention to write only a scientific account of the expedition in search of Sir John Franklin, but I persuaded him to make of it the popular narrative he did, and he afterwards admitted to me that I was right in my suggestion."

A second book that coined money for the firm was by "Parson Brownlow." Fifty thousand copies were ordered in advance of publication. This second success made the firm of Childs & Peterson the wonder of the book publishing world; everybody realized that some one connected with the house had a remarkable ability to forecast the taste of the people. This feeling was intensified when to these first successes were added "Peterson's Familiar Science," of which a quarter of a million copies were sold; Dr. Allibone's "Dictionary of British and American Authors," the first three volumes of which cost sixty thousand dollars, and several other popular treatises.

Thirteen years as a publisher brought Mr. Childs to the time when he could undertake to carry out the dream of years, the publication of the *Public Ledger*. This was in 1864. Learning that the paper, which had always been sold for a penny, was rapidly losing money, owing to the fact that the purchasing power of a penny was not what it had been before the war, he told his friends of his purpose of buying the property. They earnestly advised him not to be so foolish; they said that a property which was running behind one hundred and fifty thousand dollars a year was not a good investment.

But he saw his chance to make of the newspaper a paying business. He had more courage than the old proprietors, who dared not increase the price of subscription and advertising, so he was able to buy the property for little more than the amount of its annual loss.

How events justified the judgment of Mr. Childs was afterward told in his own words:

"The *Ledger* was purchased December 3, 1864. A week later I announced two simple but radical changes. I doubled the price of the paper, and advanced the advertising rates to a profitable figure. Of course there was an instant and not inconsiderable falling off of patronage. But the *Ledger* was already an 'institution' of the city; for twenty years it had been the established medium of communication between employers and employed, between buyers and sellers, landlords and tenants, bereaved families and their friends.

To very many people it was a necessity. So, although at first I lost some subscribers and advertisers, they were soon won back again. At the end of a month the price of the *Ledger* was reduced from twelve to ten cents a week, and from that day to this the circulation and advertising have increased."

But this result was not achieved without the hardest of hard work. For several years he seldom left the editorial rooms before midnight, averaging from twelve to fourteen hours a day at the office. He gave his personal attention to everything that appeared in the columns, and succeeded in his purpose to elevate the tone of what had been considered as a clean family paper. One who observed his methods said:

" Mr. Childs excluded all details of disgusting crime; all reports of such vice as may not with propriety be read aloud in the family, that poison the minds of young men, inflame the passions, and corrupt the heart; all scandals and slang, and that whole class of news which constitutes the staple of many daily papers. The same rule was applied to the advertising columns, and from them was excluded all that, in any shape or form, might be offensive to good morals. The friends of the new publisher predicted an early and total failure, . . . but he was governed in his course by two considerations: first, he had his own strong convictions of what is right, and secondly, a strong conviction of

what would pay; and it has been well said that
when one's ideas of duty coincide with his pecuniary interests, all the faculties work in perfect
harmony. The effect of this sudden change was,
at first, to sink the sinking concern still lower. A
class of readers and advertisers fell off. A less
conscientious and a less courageous man would
have staggered in the path he had marked out. Not
so Mr. Childs. He employed the best talent, and
paid fair wages for good work. He published six
days in the week only, and on the seventh day he
rested from his labours. His hope and his principles began to obtain recognition in the city. He
made it a family journal. It gained the confidence
of the best people who became its daily readers, and
therefore it was sought as the best medium of
advertising."

On June 20, 1867—less than three years after
the newspaper was purchased—a new building,
fully equipped for the work of an up-to-date newspaper, was opened. In planning the rooms, Mr.
Childs had in mind the comfort of those who were
to work there, feeling not only that they were en-
titled to consideration for their own sake, but that
the interests of the establishment demanded satisfied and happy employes.

Always his relations with his employes were
most pleasant. He thought of their interests, and
they in turn thought of his. It was once written
of him: " He refused to reduce the rate of pay-

ment of his compositors, although the Typographical Union had formally sanctioned a reduction, and although the reduced scale was operative in every printing office in Philadelphia except his own. He said, ' My business is prosperous, why should not my men share in my prosperity?' For many years he paid his printers in the aggregate over ten thousand dollars a year more than the union rate required, or more than he need have paid. This act of graciousness, while it endeared him to the hearts of his beneficiaries, was commented on most favorably at home and abroad. That his employes, in a formal interview with him, expressed their willingness to accept the reduced rate, simply augments the generosity of his act."

The writer of a sketch of Mr. Child's life said: " Each person in his employ has a summer vacation of two or more weeks, his wages being continued meantime, and paid in advance, with a liberal sum besides. (This was long before the right of a workman to a vacation with pay was recognized.) On Christmas every man, woman and boy receives a present, amounting to many hundreds of pounds annually. Mr. Childs has taken care of many who have become old or disabled in his service." The foreman of his composing room, who had worked for him less than twelve months before he failed in health, drew his pay weekly for years, until his death.

A year after the completion of the building

where such pleasant quarters were provided for his employes, Mr. Childs bought a large plot in one of the most beautiful cemeteries of Philadelphia, which was dedicated to the use of printers who might wish to rest there. The first man whose body was buried in this plot was a printer who died in the poor-house.

Mr. Childs was interested in prolonging the lives of printers, as well as in providing for their comfort in work, and their burial. By a munificent gift, he founded in Colorado Springs a home for employes of his own and other printing establishments who survive the years when they feel ready for active life. There hundreds of men have ended their days in comfort.

It is not strange, then, that the name of the printer's friend was honoured from the Atlantic to the Pacific. Once a labor leader who was studying labor conditions in Virginia mentioned his name to the president of the local organization of compositors. "Oh, sir," said he, as his face brightened with loving gratitude, "if all employers were like Mr. George W. Childs, there would be no labor question."

On one occasion, when the employes of the *Ledger* gave a banquet to him, one of them said: "The thing in him that is plainest to me is that there is less of evil in him than in any man I ever knew. No one can say that he went to him with a tale of true sorrow and went away empty-handed.

He overlooks our shortcomings in the *Ledger* office, and many of us have done that which might be cause for dismissal from other establishments. But we are all there, still at work, because he could not frame his lips to say the word that would cause our departure."

In all his dealings with his employes he lived up to the motto which he announced when he bought the *Public Ledger:* " Meanness is not necessary to success in business, but economy is." He insured the lives of many of his employes; he founded a pension system for them, making them feel that this was a part of their wages, not a charity. Yet, in spite of his disclaimers, the public persisted in thinking of these provisions for others as large-hearted philanthropy.

He had a large part in securing for Philadelphia Fairmount Park, one of the largest and most beautiful recreation grounds in the world. At the edge of the park are the famous Zoological Gardens, which are also a monument to him, among others who were inspired by him to plan for this educational resort. When the Centennial Exposition of 1876 was first talked of, he was one of the earliest and largest subscribers.

But many of his gifts were made so quietly that they were known only to his pastor or to those who benefited by them. He did not seek publicity for his gifts. Such benefactions as his annual dinner to the newsboys of the city and his free excursion

to the poor children were known far and wide, but
the general public never heard of the families
whose poverty he relieved, or the ambitious
students whom he helped to an education.

Gifts were not confined to America. On October 17, 1887, the beautiful George W. Childs
Memorial to Shakespeare was dedicated at
Stratford-upon-Avon, "the most imposing archi-
tectural monument erected in any country to the
genius of Shakespeare." The purpose of the donor
was to draw still closer together the cousins on both
sides of the sea. When he learned the wish of
Dean Stanley, of Westminster, to place a memorial
window in the Abbey to George Herbert and William Cowper, as Westminster Schoolboys, he
"spontaneously and large-heartedly expressed his
readiness to furnish such a window at his own
cost." The offer was accepted, and the window
was duly installed. On receiving a letter from his
friend, Archdeacon Farrar, in which the writer
spoke of his regret that there was no appropriate
memorial in England to the poet Milton, except
that in Westminster Abbey, Mr. Childs offered to
place in St. Margaret's church a memorial window
of fitting design.

It is not strange that the philanthropist who was
so well loved on both sides of the sea should be
mentioned for the Presidency. In 1888, from
many sources, pressure was brought to bear on him
to allow his name to be used as a candidate. In-

fluential papers offered their support, and large gifts were volunteered for a campaign fund. Printers and publishers all over the country hailed the suggestion with delight, and the disappointment was great when Mr. Childs said that it would be impossible for him to stand for the office, or to accept even if he were elected. He was well content to serve his fellows in private life.

During the last twenty years of his life his home in Philadelphia sheltered famous people from all parts of the world. Literary men from England and America were his guests. Dom Pedro, of Brazil, spent some days with him, the first time the emperor was ever the guest of a private citizen. Once a writer of a magazine article on his life said that the list of his world-famous guests would fill several pages of the magazine.

In 1890 *Harper's Weekly* said of the Philadelphia philanthropist:

" It was long ago said of Mr. George W. Childs that he was the two Cheeryble Brothers rolled into one; but probably a more appropriate name for him would be the Santa Claus of the newspaper world. On his last Christmas Day Mr. Childs, it is said, gave presents amounting to many thousand dollars in hard cash to the editors, reporters, compositors, pressmen and other employes of the *Ledger*. When it is considered that the salaries and wages paid by him are larger than the largest paid by other Philadelphia publishers, it will be recognized that any one associated with him in his work has cause to be satisfied with his employer. It is said by his employes, however, that they have even greater cause for satisfaction with him because of his daily consideration for them than for his Christmas bounty. It is represented to be pretty much of the same admirable sort as that of Mr. Fuzziwig for his employes, which was so warmly described by Scrooge. 'He has the power,' said old Jacob Marley's partner, 'to make us happy or unhappy, to make our service light or burdensome, a pleasure or a toil. Say that his power lies in words and looks, in things so slight and insignificant that it is impossible to add and count 'em up; what then? The happiness he gives is quite as great as if it cost a fortune.' That is said to describe with wondrous accuracy Mr. Childs' relations with his employes, who say he is a man who honours Christmas in his heart, and keeps it always."

When the Philadelphia *Record* reprinted this appreciation, it made the comment, "True—every word of it." And the New York *Star* said, "And hundreds of men in all parts of the world will confirm it."

On Feb. 3, 1894, when this great man died, the whole city wept for him, and thousands in many lands joined Philadelphians in their grief that his life on earth was done, and in joy that the world had known him for so many years.

XI

The Making of a Historian

The Story of George Bancroft's Progress

"THEIR breakfast consisted of rye bread tosted, the fragments of cold coffee boyled and put on milk. At dinner my children always dined with us—cheap soup or pudding would be generally seen. I learn'd many cheap dishes and made them satisfactory to my family."

This picture of the plain living in the boyhood home of George Bancroft, who was born October 3, 1800, shows how limited were the means of his father, the minister of one of the churches of Worcester, Massachusetts. But as it was always the rule of the household to keep out of debt, no matter how scant the supply of money, the family managed to get along well.

Of one thing there was not a scant supply—love. Father and mother and children loved one another so much that they forgot the hardships. As the mother added to the statement concerning the food: " I always did it with my own hands, they as cheerful and satisfied as if it was a dainty, for why? Because mother gave it to them."

Both father and mother had been acquainted with poverty in their youth, so they were the better able to care for their children without incurring debt. The father's home living had been severely plain, and the mother had seen the furniture in her childhood home sold for debt, even the chair on which her mother sat being sold from under her.

But while Mr. Bancroft was unable to give his thirteen children many worldly advantages, he could train them to read and think. In his library were many historical volumes, heirlooms from his own father; these were studied with care. George, especially, was attracted by them. The father's own tastes were for historical work, as was shown by his Life of Washington, written in 1807, of which several editions were called for. The volume revealed his ability to think for himself, an ability he proposed to teach to his children. His wise way with them George remembered and described when he was an old man:

" Whenever members of his family consulted him on a question of belief, he never taught them by his own authority, but would set before them arguments on each side, and recommended to them the best writers on the subject; he really wished them to arrive at their own conclusions by their own unbiased reflection."

Of the ten children in that home who lived through childhood two sons died at sea. One daughter became the wife of a governor of Massachusetts, another became the mother of an admiral of the United States Navy, while the third helped her brother George, the future historian, with his manuscripts and proof. One of his brothers became a judge of distinction, while another was noted as a general in the army. M. A. De Wolfe Howe, the biographer of the most famous member of the family, well says:

"The rye bread tosted, the fragments of cold coffee boyled and put on milk were dispensed by the happy mother to a rarely potential group of children."

In looking back at his own boyhood, George did not speak of himself in flattering terms. Later in life he wrote to a cousin of one of the playmates of his boyhood:

"I was a wild boy, and your aunt did not like me. She was always fearful that I would get her son into bad ways, and still more alarmed lest I should some day be the cause of his being brought home dead. There was a river, or piece of water, near Worcester, where I used to beguile young Salisbury, and having constructed a rude sort of raft, he and I would pass a good deal of our playtime in aquatic amusements, not by any means unattended by danger. Madame's remonstrances were all in vain, and she was more and more confirmed in the opinion that I was a wild, bad boy. However, nothing beyond an occasional wetting ever occurred, yet I never rose in her estimation and a ' wild boy ' I continued to be up to manhood."

When he was six years old, his father turned to him and asked him to settle a disputed point in Roman history, Chief Justice Parsons being one of the disputants!

To his father belonged the credit for training him in history, as well as in other subjects, for his school privileges were most meager. The school he attended was two miles from his father's farm, and during the three years he went there the instruction given hardly paid for the walk.

When he was eleven years old he left home to attend Phillips Academy, in Exeter, New Hampshire. Although so young, he was as far advanced as his classmates. He made good use of his opportunities, rejoicing that because of the scholarship given him he could share in benefits which otherwise would have been impossible. His pocket was usually empty. During the two years he remained at the Academy he was unable to make the short journey to his father's house.

A friend of his father who visited Exeter during his stay there wrote to Mr. Bancroft that the principal said "he was a very fine lad; that he appeared to have the stamina of a distinguished man; that he took his rank among the first scholars in the academy; and that he wished I would send him half a dozen such boys."

One of the deepest impressions made on his

mind at this period was during a visit to Portsmouth where he heard Daniel Webster, then comparatively unknown, make an oration on July 4, 1812. He never forgot the orator. When he was an old man he said that Webster made no " gesture whatever except that once he placed his right hand over his heart." It is difficult to decide whether to admire more the man who made such an indelible impression on a boy of twelve, or the boy who observed so carefully and remembered so accurately.

His great ambition when at Exeter was to carry off one of the prizes offered for excellence in the work of each year. To the friend with whom he spent the vacation in Portsmouth he said he feared he would not succeed, for in the academy there were only two younger than himself. But he resolved to try. And he succeeded. In the history of the academy it is recorded that he " carried off the prize of four dollars, as the scholar who most distinguished himself in constancy and parsing the Greek and Latin languages."

He was not yet thirteen when he entered Harvard College. When he was a little more than fourteen he wrote what is the earliest known specimen from his pen. Having been given the Latin theme, " Dimidium facti, qui cœpit, habet," he started out:

" In this sententious maxim Horace, the Prince of lyrick poetry, presented to our view the difficulty of beginning. But why is it as arduous to begin as to complete an enterprise?"

When fourteen years and six months old he was asked to write on "Reading," and he made this comparison between a popular boy's book of the day and the volume for which his academy prize money had been spent:

"The wonderful exploits of a visionary hero excite a deeper interest than the brilliant action of illustrious generals; and many are delighted with the beauties of the 'Scottish Chiefs,' while they derive no pleasure from 'Christian Morals.'"

He was not quite seventeen when he graduated near the head of his class. To him was given a leading part in the commencement exercises. He spoke "on the dignity and utility of philosophy of the human mind," and declared:

"The man who has been introduced to the wonders and glories and pleasures of intellect feels himself elevated above the common sphere of mankind. He lives in an upper world and contemplates with calm indifference the labours of ordinary men as of inferior beings, like the majestick eagle, who, heedless of the croakings of the ravens below, rises on ample wing,

> 'Sailing with supreme dominion
> Through the azure deep of air.'"

On June 27, 1818, the young student sailed for

Germany, where he planned to do post-graduate work in preparation for the ministry, the necessary funds being provided by Harvard College and by friends who believed in him. Assured of seven hundred dollars per year, he felt rich.

The austere manner of his life at Göttingen he pictured in an early letter to his mother:

" I rise before five in the morning, though in this high Northern region the sun does not get up till very late. On rising I find my stove already warm and the room comfortable, and a pot of coffee on the table. I drink at once a cup of this, and so on at intervals of half an hour till all is gone. At seven I go to my drawer and cut me from my brown loaf a piece of bread and butter. This lasts until dinner, which is brought to me, and is a solitary meal. After dinner the Germans drink coffee again. The evening is the time for visits. . . . If one will study, however, in the evening, bread and butter and a cup of tea is his repast, and he can labour very well on a light stomach."

He allowed himself six hours for sleep, and mapped out the remainder of the twenty-four hours, so that sixteen hours were devoted to study, and two hours to walking and eating! In this he followed the advice of a professor who urged him to study hard, adding that no man naturally possessed of a good constitution ever died of study.

After two years the course leading to the doctor's degree was completed, and he set out for

Berlin for further study. It is evident that he had
fallen into the bad habit meantime of rising later
than six o'clock, for on January 1, 1821, he
resolved:

" To rise earlier than I have formerly done.
Half past five or six is a proper hour for winter,
except when something unusual prevents me from
going to bed in good season."

Study at Heidelberg and at Paris followed.
One of the most memorable experiences in Paris
was a walking excursion with Washington Irving,
who gave him advice that he long remembered:

" At my time of life, he tells me, I ought to lay
aside all cares, and only be bent on laying in a
stock of knowledge for future application. If I
have not pecuniary resources enough to get at what
I could wish for, as calculated to be useful to my
mind, I must still not give up the pursuit. Still
follow it; scramble to it; get at it as you can, but be
sure to get at it. If you need books, buy them; if
you are in want of instruction in anything, take it.
The time will come soon when it will be too late
for these things."

The crown was put to his student days by a long
walking tour over the Alps and into Italy. This
was one of the happiest experiences of his life.
The beauties of the landscape gave him keenest
joy. One day he wrote:

" I was seized with delight, and though worn
with a long walk, could not but caper and sing or at

least cry out a chorus of a rude song, as I passed amidst such beautiful scenes. I danced and sported and sprang about and might well have been taken for a madman."

The contrast between the beauties without and his own wayworn appearance was impressed on him one day. In a letter he said:

"For a long time I have not looked in a mirror, and as I glanced my eye at one this morning I was frightened at my own long black beard. I wonder I have not been taken for a madman. My socks are all worn out, my trousers are going, my shoes are good for nothing, my coat is decaying, my money is nearly spent."

In August, 1822, he was in America once more. When the fall term of Harvard College opened he became a tutor of Greek. He had not given up his plan for the ministry, but delayed the completion of his course. During the winter he preached many times in the leading churches of Boston and vicinity.

In 1823 he definitely turned his back on the ministry. In that year he opened a boys' preparatory school at Northampton, Massachusetts, where he taught with much success till 1831. But his heart was more engaged in writing than in teaching. To the volume of poems which he published in 1823 he added half a dozen volumes on the classics and history, and wrote many articles for the *North American Review*.

Four years before leaving the school he was

married.   Ten years later his wife died, leaving in the home two sons and a daughter.

After turning aside from teaching he gave his attention to politics as well as literature.   In 1834 he was a Democratic candidate for the General Court, but, fortunately, he was badly defeated. The Boston *Courier* commented on the event:

" We rejoice that Mr. Bancroft was defeated, though we are sorry that he is obliged to suffer the mortification that follows it.   We hope that he has learned a useful and salutary lesson; and that he will turn from the wilderness of politics into which he plunged so inconsiderately, to the more attract-ive garden of literature—a field which he can culti-vate, enrich and adorn—imparting profit and pleas-ure to his country, and reaping honour to himself. We advise him—no, advice he would think im-pertinent—we hope, and entreat, in the spirit of friendship, that he will write no more letters to the *Workingman* (the paper in which he had told his principles) . . . at least till he shall have com-pleted his history of the United States.   That, if finished as begun, will be a testimony to his talents and fame, more enduring and more grateful to his descendants, than all the honours he can ever ac-quire as a politician."

Bancroft did not see fit to follow this advice. For years he remained among the politicians.   In 1844 he came within fifteen thousand votes of being elected Governor of Massachusetts.

The first volume of the History, which appeared in 1834, attracted widespread attention and hearty approval. Historians realized that the writer was a man of might, and that his ambitious work would become a classic. He was commended for his thoroughness, his originality, and the readableness of his work. Edward Everett wrote to him: " You give us not wretched pasteboard men; not a sort of chronological table, with the dates written out at length, after the manner of most historians;—but you give us real, individual, living men and women, with their passions, interests and peculiarities."

Before the second volume was published he was appointed Collector of the Port of Boston, then the most important post of the kind in the country. His position gave him an ample income for his needs while continuing the work of writing. But the tasks of the office were not neglected for literature. It is matter of record that the duties were better performed by him than by any of his predecessors. One of the notable acts of his administration was the appointment of Nathaniel Hawthorne to a post in the Custom House.

Four years after the close of his term as collector came his appointment as Secretary of the Navy in the cabinet of President James K. Polk. Soon after the beginning of his services he had another opportunity to help Hawthorne, who was living in poverty. His recommendation that the author of " Twice Told Tales " be appointed Surveyor of the Port of Salem was favorably received by the Senate.

Though Bancroft continued in the cabinet only a year and a half, he outlined the plan of the Naval Academy at Annapolis. Before becoming Minister to England he saw the institution in working order. Thus he accomplished what his predecessors had tried for thirty years to bring about.

Service at the Court of St. James, and later service as minister to Germany, gave him ample opportunity to search for material for his history, which he was able to complete as far as the beginning of the country's independent existence. His first plan had been to make a complete history, but the magnitude of the task and his conscientious work made this impossible.

While the History was his chief literary work, other books of permanent value were published during the last forty years of his life.

It was January 17, 1891, when he died. Two days later President Harrison issued the proclamation:

" As an expression of the public loss and sorrow, the flags of all the executive departments at Washington and of the public buildings in the cities through which the funeral party is to pass will be placed at half-mast on to-morrow and until the body of this eminent statesman, scholar and historian shall finally rest in the state that gave him to his country and the world."

XII

The Making of a Naturalist

*The Boyhood Experiences and Inventions of
John Muir*

"BAIRNS, you needna learn your lessons the nicht, for we're gane to America the morn!"

The startling message came to John Muir one evening in 1849 as he was studying with his brother David in the home in Dunbar, Scotland, where he was born April 21, 1838.

At once he was wild with excitement. It had always been his delight to live in the fields and the woods, among the birds and the animals. The strict laws forbidding trespassing and poaching had made him listen with wonder to the tales of the free life in the new world. Visions of delight came to him.

" No more grammar, but boundless woods full of mysterious good things; trees, full of sugar, growing in ground full of gold; hawks, eagles, pigeons, filling the sky; millions of birds' nests, and no gamekeepers to stop us in all the wild happy land."

But his grandfather, who listened to his raptures, tried to open his eyes to the truth.

"Ah, poor laddy, poor laddy, you'll find something else ower the sea forbye gold and sugar, birds' nests and freedom fra lessons and school. You'll find plenty hard, hard work."

And so it proved, of course. Mr. Muir took his family to a claim in Wisconsin. The first home was a log shanty, built in the woods, by the help of the neighbors, in less than a day.

The boys' explorations began before the ox-team, which hauled the household goods to the clearing, heard the welcome command to come to a stand. First they climbed a tree in which they saw the nest of a bird.

"Then we ran along the brow of the hill that the shanty stood on," Mr. Muir wrote a half century later, "and down to the meadow, searching the trees and the grass tufts and bushes, and soon discovered a bluebird's and a woodpecker's nest, and began an acquaintance with the frogs and snakes and turtles in the creeks and springs. This sudden flash into free wilderness—baptism in Nature's warm heart—how happy it made us! Nature streaming into us, wooingly teaching her wonderful glowing lessons, so unlike the dismal grammar ashes and cinders so long thrashed out to us. Here, without knowing it, we were still at school, every wild lesson a love lesson, not whipped but charmed into us. Oh, that glorious Wisconsin wilderness!

Everything new and pure in the very prime of the spring when Nature's pulses were beating highest and mysteriously keeping time with our own! Young hearts, young leaves, flowers, animals, the winds and the streams and the sparkling lake, all wildly, gladly rejoicing together!"

The story of the years spent on that Wisconsin farm, as told by Mr. Muir in "My Boyhood and Youth," gives a wonderful glimpse into the heart of a boy who loved Nature and saw in every leaf and flower and bird and animal evidences of the love of God. Year by year delight increased. The farm never seemed a lonely place, companionship was always to be found in the woods or the fields.

Free time for observation was scarce, but John made the most of his working hours. For him the days were filled with pleasure because he knew how to enjoy his surroundings while he toiled. In the woods when he cut rails for the seemingly interminable fences, the trees whispered to him their secrets, the birds charmed him by their songs, and the woods creatures became his familiar friends. When he was guiding the heavy plow and turning up the sod that had never before been broken the smell of the earth and even the great roots of the clearing that many times threatened to throw him from his feet, had a language which to him was not a foreign tongue.

He did not lack for opportunities to use the axe or guide the plow. At both tasks he soon became such an adept that his father was well content to turn to other duties, leaving these to the sturdy youth. As soon as the first claim was fenced, a half section near by was bought and he had to begin the back-breaking work of providing material for the new fences.

"The trees that were tall enough and straight enough to afford one or two logs ten feet long were used for rails, the others, too knotty or cross-grained, were disposed of in log and cord wood fences. I used to cut and split a hundred rails a day from our short, knotty oak timber, swinging the axe and heavy mallet, often with sore hands, from early morning to night. I rather liked it, for I was proud of my skill, and tried to believe that I was as tough as the timber I mauled, though this and other heavy jobs stopped my growth and earned me the title, 'Runt of the family.' "

When nineteen years old John was the acknowledged expert plowman of the neighborhood. With ease and accuracy he could handle a plow which turned a furrow from eighteen inches to two feet wide, and drawn by four or five yoke of oxen. It was necessary to have so much power because the ground when first plowed was underlaid with the tap roots of oak and hickory bushes, called "gouts," some of which were four or five inches in diameter. "If in good trim, the plow cut through and turned over these gouts as if the century-old wood were soft like the flesh of carrots and turnips, but if not in good trim the grubs promptly tossed the plow out of the ground." The Muir plow was kept in such good condition, and John was so skillful that, after getting started on a new furrow, he was "able to ride on the cross-bar between the handles, his feet resting comfortably on the beam, without having to steady or steer it in any way on the whole length of the field," unless it was necessary to go round a stump.

On the second farm there was no water, not even a small spring. So a well was to be dug, and John was expected to do the work. For ten feet progress was easy. Then fine-grained sandstone was struck. It was found impracticable to blast the rock, so Mr. Muir asked his son to use mason's chisels.

"I had to sit cramped in a space about three feet in diameter," he has said in describing the work, "and wearily chip, chip with heavy hammer and chisels from early morning until dark, day after day, for weeks and months. In the morning, father and David lowered me in a wooden bucket by a windlass, hauled up what chips were left from the night before, then went away to the farm work and left me until noon, when they hoisted me out for dinner. After dinner I was promptly lowered again, the forenoon's accumulation of chips hoisted out of the way, and I was left until night."

One morning, when the well was about eighty feet deep, the workman was all but suffocated by

choke-damp. His father, waiting for the waste
chips, asked him why he kept so still. The voice
roused him from his lethargy, but he could only
shout feebly, " Take me out." A neighbor, who
had been a miner, congratulated him on his narrow
escape, and told him how to avoid future difficulty,
by lowering, before descending, a lighted candle,
which would not burn if gas were present; by
throwing water down the shaft to absorb the gas;
and by dropping a bundle of brush or hay attached
to a light rope, dropping it again and again to
carry down free air and stir up the poison.

Ten feet more of chipping through the sandstone
was completed before there was the welcome gush
of water. Then the store chamber filled with
water, and for years the family rejoiced as they
made use of the two buckets which went up and
down the shaft, which was straight and plumb as it
was possible to make it, though, as Mr. Muir
proudly said, " father never spent an hour in that
well."

There was no opportunity to attend school during this Wisconsin boyhood, except once for a brief
term. At first John did not object; he was glad to
be free from the slavery of lessons. But when he
was fifteen he asked his father to buy for him a
higher arithmetic, and he began to study at home.
In one summer he finished the book without assistance, " in the short intervals between the end of
dinner and the afternoon start for the field." In

the same way he studied algebra, geometry, and trigonometry, and reviewed the detested grammar.

His father did not encourage general reading. He owned a few books of a very solid character; these his sons were free to read. But he looked askance at the borrowing of books from neighbors, especially such dreadful books as Scott's novels! Yet he began to buy a little library for himself. He was able to secure a few dollars; these he spent for the poetry of Shakespeare, Milton, Cowper, Henry Kirk White, Campbell and Akenside.

The hunger for reading brought him to the turning point of his life. Thus he has told the story:

"There was desperately little time for reading, even in the winter evenings—only a few stolen minutes now and then. Father's strict rule was, straight to bed, immediately after family worship, which in winter was usually over by eight o'clock. I was in the habit of lingering in the kitchen with a book and candle after the rest of the family had retired, and considered myself fortunate if I got five minutes' reading before father noticed the light and ordered me to bed; an order that of course I immediately obeyed. But night after night I tried to steal minutes in the same lingering way, and how keenly precious those minutes were, few nowadays can know. Father failed perhaps two or three times in a whole winter to notice my light for nearly ten minutes—magnificent, golden blocks of time, long to be remembered like holidays or geo-

logical periods. One evening when I was reading
church history father was particularly irritable, and
called out with hope-killing emphasis, ' John, go to
bed! Must I give you a separate order every night
to get you to go to bed? Now, I will have no ir-
regularity in the family; you must go when the
rest go, and without my having to tell you.' Then,
as an afterthought, as if judging that his words
and tone of voice were too severe for so pardon-
able an offense as reading a religious book, he un-
warily added: ' If you will read, get up in the
morning and read. You may get up in the morning as early as you like.' "

That was all the ambitious boy needed. Usually
his sleep was unbroken, but that night he woke
before his father called him. Hurrying on his
clothes, he went with his candle to the kitchen
clock, only to discover that it was just one o'clock!

Then what? Back to bed? Never! " I had
gained five hours, almost half a day. ' Five hours
to myself!' I said. ' Five huge, solid hours!' I
can hardly think of any other event of my life, any
discovery I ever made that gave birth to joy so
transporting glorious as the possession of these five
frosty hours."

His first thought was to use the precious hours
for reading. But the night was very cold, and he
would need a fire. Fearing that his father would
object to his burning stovewood for such a useless
occupation as reading, he decided that it would be

wise to give the time to the completion of a self-setting saw-mill he had invented. So that morning, and for many mornings following, he went to the cellar where he had fitted up his work bench. He needed more tools than the few owned by his father, so he made a fine-toothed saw out of a strip of corset steel, and fashioned his own brad-awls, punches, and a pair of compasses, using wire and old files for the purpose.

Two weeks passed before Mr. Muir said a word. But the noise under his bed disturbed him so much that at length he found fault. Respectfully his son reminded him that he had given his permission to rise early; he knew that his father had the Scotchman's regard for his word.

"I know it," was the agonized answer. "I know I gave you that miserable permission, but I never imagined you would get up in the middle of the night."

When the saw-mill was done a stream was dammed and it was put in operation. It worked so well that the inventor determined to give more of his precious hours to machinery instead of to his beloved books. In succession he made " water-wheels, curious doorlocks and latches, thermometers, hygrometers, pyrometers, clocks, a barometer, an automatic contrivance for feeding the horses at any required time, a lamplighter and firelighter, an early-or-late rising machine, and so forth."

When he conceived the ambitious project of constructing a clock that "would tell the day of the week, and the day of the month, as well as strike like a common clock and point out the hours," and to have "an attachment whereby it could be connected with a bedstead to set me on my feet at any hour in the morning, also to start fires, light lamps, etc.," he had never seen the inside of a clock or a watch. However, he had studied in a book the laws of the pendulum. After carefully thinking out the parts, these were made of wood and put together, and the mechanism did everything he had planned.

Another clock had a hand, pointed with a star, which rose and set with the sun the year round. A thermometer, made of an old rod from a wagon bed, was constructed and fixed on the side of the house, which was so large that it could be read by workmen in the field, and so sensitive that the needle would move perceptibly when an observer approached within four or five feet, thus warming the atmosphere.

Mrs. Muir wished to see her son a minister, but when she saw how his heart was set on inventions she urged him to go into a machine shop. He tried to find an opening, but failed. Then she suggested that he take several of his inventions to the State Fair; perhaps some one would see them who would give him the opening he sought.

When he left home his father offered him no

money, but told him to depend on himself. He had fifteen dollars of his own. With this small fund, and a package in which were " two clocks and a small thermometer made of a piece of old washboard—all three tied together, with no covering or case of any sort "—he set out for Madison. He was a little down-hearted, fearing, as he said, that people would not care to look at things made of wood. But his father's encouraging words rang in his ear. " Made of wood! Made of wood! What does it matter what things are made of when they are so out-and-out original? There's nothing else like them in the world. That is what will attract attention, and besides they're mighty handsome things anyway, to come from the backwoods."

Everywhere he went the inventions attracted attention. The conductor of the train on which he took passage advised him to leave them with the baggage master, or curious travelers would be apt to break them. Then he persuaded the engineer to grant the young man's request to be allowed to ride on the locomotive. But he was not content in the cab. A locomotive was a strange thing to him, so he asked permission to explore. Then he surprised the engineer by his fearlessness.

" I went out and walked along the foot-board on the side of the boiler, watching the magnificent machine rushing through the landscape, as if glorying in its strength like a living creature. While seated on the cow-catcher platform, I seemed to be fairly flying, and the wonderful display of power and motion was enchanting. This was the first time I had been on a train, much less a locomotive, since I left Scotland."

At the fair his inventions were received with acclaim, and he had no difficulty in securing a place with another inventor. This proved to be unsatisfactory, so he started out for himself, manufacturing, for sale, bedsteads that set the sleepers on their feet in the morning, the motive power being a dollar alarm clock set in the foot-board.

Then came the ambition to go to the state university. Four years he spent there, frequently living on half a dollar a week, supporting himself by what he earned during vacation and during term time. One winter he taught school and made of his clock a servant to light the fire at eight o'clock in the morning. His plan was to place a teaspoonful of powdered chlorate of potash and sugar on the stove-hearth near a few shavings and kindling, and at the required time make the clock touch the inflammable mixture with a drop of sulphuric acid.

For his use at college he invented a desk of marvelous sort:

"The books I had to study were arranged in order at the beginning of each term. I also made a bed which set me on my feet every morning at the hour determined on, and in dark winter mornings, just as the bed set me on the floor it lighted a lamp. Then, after the minutes allowed for dressing had elapsed a click was heard, and the first book to be studied was pushed up from a rack below the top of the desk, thrown open, and allowed to remain there the number of minutes required. Then the machinery closed the book and allowed it to drop back into its stall, then moved the rack forward and threw up the next in order, and so on, all the day being divided according to the time of recitation, and time required and allotted to each study."

In summer the bed was operated by sun power. Taking a lens out of a spy glass, he fixed this on the window sill. The sunbeam focused through this on a thread, burned it through, and so released the bed machinery.

After leaving college he was threatened with total blindness, and he determined first to see as much of the world as possible. On foot he went southward, sleeping in the open air, gathering botanical specimens as he went. When in Indianapolis he ran out of funds, and agreed to operate a wood-working shop during the proprietor's absence for a year. When the owner returned and found that, through his helper's inventions, the work of the shop was being done at half the expense considered necessary at the beginning, he offered to make him a partner. But Mr. Muir was determined to continue his journey.

By way of the Isthmus of Panama he went to San Francisco. The city did not attract him. He wanted to go to the Sierra Nevada Mountains.

" Where is the Sierra Nevada? " he asked a man on the street.

" Over yonder," was the reply.

So " over yonder " he went, walking one hundred miles to the mountains which, all the rest of his life, he called home.

Within a few years he knew the mountains thoroughly. He tramped over every foot of the Yosemite, and was instrumental in persuading Congress to set aside the Yosemite National Park.

It was his habit to carry no luggage as he went into the wilderness. His only burden, carried on his back, was a tin cup, a packet of tea, a sack of bread, and a hand-axe. He never carried a tent or even blankets.

Money was earned for a year's supplies by a month or two of work on a valley farm. Then supplies were bought, and preparation made for another year's disappearance.

Then he set up a saw-mill among the Big Trees that he might earn money as he studied the glories about him. He lived in the attic of the mill. In all the years of his ownership of the place he cut only fallen timber.

When he had saved five hundred dollars, or enough for two years' expenses, he gave up the mill and went to San Francisco to buy supplies. There he met her who became his wife. The wedding trip was taken to the Yosemite—and the money was all spent.

In 1881 he joined the *Courier* expedition in search of the Jeannette party, lost in the Arctic. While in Alaskan waters he discovered the great glacier which bears his name. Later he went on a world-tour to study trees, and managed to penetrate into forests where none but a native of the country had ever been before.

But always he preferred the Sierras as his home. From there he wrote most of the articles and books that made him famous. And from there, when invited several times to become professor in Eastern universities, he sent the message:

" There are already too many men teaching the things they have got out of books. What we need are original investigators to write new books."

As an original investigator he continued his work until his death in 1914.

XIII

From a Country Store to the President's Chair

The Rapid Rise of Grover Cleveland

ONE night toward the close of the first half of the nineteenth century the residents of the quiet village of Fayetteville, New York, heard the insistent pealing of the academy bell. They thought something must surely be wrong; perhaps it was a fire. They must investigate. So many of the people rushed from their homes, only to return in a few minutes, uncertain whether to be angry or to laugh at the prank of fun-loving "Grover" Cleveland, who had been found with his brother William suspiciously near the bell-rope. He had decided that the time had come to make a break in the monotony of life in a small town.

Yet Fayetteville was a larger place than the Cleveland family had been accustomed to. When Stephen Grover Cleveland was born, on March 18, 1837, his father, Rev. Richard Cleveland, was pastor of the Presbyterian Church of Caldwell, New Jersey. There the first three or four years of his life were spent.

The removal to Fayetteville was one of the first

distinct memories of his boyhood, for the journey involved a trip up the Hudson as far as Albany by steamer, and then by the Erie canal boat to the point nearest the new home.

Across the street from the Fayetteville manse was a building which had great attractions for Grover, the village academy. He was informed that he might join the students there when he was old enough. In the meantime he attended the primary school, and looked with envy on the boys and girls who could enter the charmed precincts of the more aristocratic seat of learning. He saw them at their games, and it seemed to him that they had so much more fun than he. Soon it became his chief ambition to be one of the favored academy class. Many times he sought permission to pass from the school which he felt was beneath his dignity to that which he felt was the gateway to manhood. Finally, when he was eleven years old, he was given his desire. Although he was one of the youngest of the students, he was soon accepted by his companions as a splendid playmate. He enjoyed play as much as they did, yet he enjoyed study more than most of them. His father had taught him to love books, and he was able to take a place in class on an equality with those much older than he.

It was fortunate that the boy had been able to begin his experience at the academy so early, for it was only a little more than a year before he was compelled to leave school. His father's salary was small, and there were nine children in the family, five girls and four boys, Grover being fifth in order. It was necessary for him to relieve his father of his support, so when one of the deacons in the church offered to take him into his general store, the offer was accepted. He remained at work more than a year, until his father moved to Clinton, New York. He proved a faithful clerk, giving far better service than could be expected from one of his years.

He did not forget his books, but in the evenings he studied diligently. Thus when the chance came to enter the preparatory department of Hamilton College, at Clinton, he was ready to take his place with boys whose schooling had never been interrupted.

Just before his brief experience in the preparatory school he had another glimpse of the world. On the bank of the Niagara River, near Buffalo, his uncle, Lewis F. Allen, had a large stock farm, and he was told he might go there for a visit. A sum sufficient for his modest needs for the round trip by canal was given him. When the time came to return home, finding that he had spent most of the money, he determined to make his own way back by the canal.

This lesson in self-reliance was helpful to him when he made up his mind that it was his duty to go to work. His application to the proprietor of the Fayetteville store in which he had clerked as a twelve-year-old boy was favorably received—evidently he had done his work well—and he was offered fifty dollars and board for the first year, this modest sum to be doubled the second year.

As before, the young clerk studied diligently whenever he could spare time from his work. At the end of the two years he hoped to return to the preparatory school, go on to college, and fit himself for professional life. But his father died, in 1853, and it was more than ever necessary that he should continue to earn money. He realized that his mother must be cared for; his father had not been able to make much provision for her needs.

William Cleveland, who was then an instructor in the Institution for the Blind at New York City, succeeded in securing for Grover temporary employment there as accountant and assistant instructor in the school. For a year he remained in this position, doing his work faithfully, broadening his mind by reading and roaming about the city, and saving for his mother every penny he could spare.

One glimpse of his New York life was given by Fanny Crosby, the blind hymn writer, in the story of her career. She told of one of her superiors in the institution who was domineering and almost insulting to her. She saw no way to compel him to treat her respectfully until Grover Cleveland, indignant because of something he had overheard, told her how to bring the tyrant to terms. She followed his advice, conditions were much improved, and she was ever after grateful to the young man who had interested himself in a helpless stranger. In her estimate of him she says, " Among other very pleasant characteristics which I noticed in him was a disposition to help others whenever possible. Knowing that it was a great favor for me to have my poems copied neatly and legibly, he offered to perform that service for me; and I several times availed myself of his aid."

He might have retained his position longer than a year, but he did not see any future for himself in the institution. He dreamed of becoming a lawyer, but he hardly knew how to set about the task of preparation. Realizing that there was no chance for him as a law student, he determined to go west as far as Cleveland, Ohio. Having resigned his position, he hurried to his mother's home at Holland Patent, New York, where he talked with her of the future. When he had her approval he sought a man in the town who had been his father's friend and asked for a loan of twenty-five dollars with which to pay the expenses of his journey to Cleveland. His request was granted, on condition that the sum lent be paid when he was able, to some other needy man, that man being put under the same obligation. Young Cleveland insisted on giving a note for the amount of the loan. In the years that followed he was not satisfied with passing it on to others, but in addition insisted on repaying the twenty-five dollars to the lender. On January 23, 1861, he wrote to his helper of early days:

" I am now in condition to pay my note which you hold, given for money borrowed some years ago. I suppose I might have paid it long before, but I have never thought you were in need of it, and I had other purposes for my money. I have forgotten the date of the note. If you will send me it, I will mail you the principal and interest. The loan you made me was my start in life, and I shall always preserve the note as an interesting reminder of your kindness."

On the way to Cleveland the ambitious young man stopped at Utica and Syracuse, hoping to find there temporary employment that would enable him to increase his expense fund. Disappointed in both places, he hastened on to Buffalo. There he made another attempt, and was more successful. The uncle whom he had visited years before urged him to study law in Buffalo; he would find a place for him in an office, and in the meantime would give him clerical work by which he could pay expenses. The uncle was compiling " The American Short Horn Herd Book," in four volumes; one volume was already out of the way, but he needed a painstaking assistant for the remaining volumes. Six years later, when the final volume was ready for the press, the compiler told in the introduction of his great indebtedness to his " friend and kinsman, Grover Cleveland, Esq., of Buffalo, a gentleman of the legal profession."

In writing of the summer on the Niagara River stock farm where the work on the second volume was done, W. O. Stoddard tells of recreations that made toil all the more enjoyable. With his cousin he went hunting and fishing, thus forming the habits of outdoor sport which were his safety valve during later strenuous years.

When fall came he was able to send to his mother sixty dollars of his earnings. She felt he would need the money himself, but he saw no reason why he could not earn his expenses as he went along.

The first application for employment in a Buffalo law office was unsuccessful. The lawyer received him so gruffly that he was discouraged. So his uncle told him he would make the next application in person. At the first attempt he was successful. He told of the smart boy at his home who was waiting for a chance to show what he could do. " Well, there's a table; tell him to come in," was the response.

Cleveland took his place at that table, and there he proposed to stay until he had made a place for himself at the bar. He was not to receive anything for his services, but he knew that his expenses were provided for, as he was to continue work for his uncle. Residence on the farm would make necessary a walk of two miles to and from the farm, but the thought did not trouble him; he knew that this would help to keep him in trim for the serious work of law study.

Work began at once. The head of the firm brought him the first volume of Blackstone's Commentaries, informing him, " That's where they all begin."

The eighteen-year-old student opened the volume and studied to some purpose. He gave himself up to his reading so completely that it was difficult to rouse him. W. O. Stoddard tells an incident of one of those strenuous early days:

" He forgot all about the time of day, and the other people in the office, lawyers and clerks, forgot all about him. They completed their tasks, locked the doors behind them and went away. Young Cleveland knew nothing of their going or of any other mundane matter but Blackstone's Commentaries, until the fading light warned him that he must tear himself away from that book. Then the locked doors informed him that for one night he was to be imprisoned, without supper, and with no better company than a large law library and the accumulated papers of the firm's extensive practice."

After a time the student began to be of value to his employer, and he was given small wages. During a part of the second year he received four dollars per week. Then his pay became large enough to warrant his leaving the farm and taking an attic room in the city. The change gave him long, uninterrupted evenings for study, and he made the most of them.

In 1858, when he was privileged to cast his first vote, he was not satisfied to leave the polls after depositing his ballot, but he remained near at hand all day, distributing Democratic tickets and making the acquaintance of the electors. This method of spending election day became a habit with him; it is said that for many years, or until public duties made the work impossible, he was a regular attendant at the polls.

In May, 1859, after four years of hard study, Mr. Cleveland was admitted to the bar. He had made himself so valuable to his employers that they asked him to take charge of the office, at a salary of six hundred dollars a year. In a little while the amount was increased to one thousand dollars; he did his work so well that he was thought to be worth far more than the average lawyer of his years. One of his associates in the office is quoted as saying of him:

" Grover won our admiration by his three traits of indomitable industry, unpretentious courage, and unswerving honesty. I never saw a more thorough man at anything he undertook. Whatever the subject was, he was reticent until he had mastered all its bearings and had made up his own mind, and then nothing could swerve him from his convictions. It was this quality of intellectual integrity more than anything else, perhaps, that made him afterward listened to and respected, when more brilliant men who were opposed to him were applauded and forgotten."

In 1863 many aspiring young lawyers in Buffalo were clamoring for appointment as assistant District Attorney. Mr. Cleveland went on with his work as usual, content that the preference should be given to others. But to the surprise of all the place was offered to him. He accepted gladly, for he knew that he would have an unusual opportunity to do effective work. His chief was not strong, and the burden would rest on him. The responsibility was great, but his performance of the duties required of him was so thoroughgoing and so conscientious that there was general satisfaction with his work. Two years later he was nominated to succeed his chief, in the hope that his personal popularity would enable his party to overcome the handicap of a disastrous campaign during the previous year. He refused to electioneer for himself, declaring that his first duty was in the court room. He ran well, but was defeated.

It was only five years till his next opportunity was thrust upon him. The Democrats of Erie County were seeking a candidate for Sheriff who would be able to bring to the party every possible vote. Without consultation with Mr. Cleveland it was decided that he was the one man for the place. Against his protest he was nominated. Election followed. For three years his energetic conduct of the office gratified the friends of good government, although it disturbed many who had been accustomed to careless methods. The six years following his term as sheriff were devoted to building up once more his law practice. For a long time his income from practice was not large. He did not have much difficulty in securing cases, but it was a different matter to secure fees. The reason was indicated by one of his partners, W. S. Bissell, when he told of closing up a case of Cleveland's which had been running on for years. During all this time Cleveland had paid all disbursements, such as costs of entry, witness fees, etc., out of his own pocket, because his client was too poor to meet these necessary expenses.

The very first case that came to him after the resumption of law practice was even more expensive to Mr. Cleveland. A poor woman sought his aid in preventing the man who held a mortgage of fourteen hundred dollars on her home from foreclosing. The lawyer, seeing that she had no case, paid the mortgage himself, and made her a gift of the amount.

His fellow citizens were not content to leave such a man in private life. In 1880 his party nominated him for Mayor of Buffalo. His first intimation of this choice came to him when a committee of notification found him in the court room. Again he had made no effort to secure the nomination.

His election was followed by honest, fearless administration that attracted the attention of the entire state and finally of the nation. Helpful, constructive legislation was demanded and secured, and vicious ordinances were vetoed with a firmness that discomfited his opponents. In sending his veto messages he was not afraid of plain speech. Once he said:

" I withhold my assent because I regard this as the culmination of a most bare-faced, impudent, and shameless scheme to betray the interests of the people, and to worse than squander the public money."

The next step in the surprising advance of Mr. Cleveland was taken when, in 1882, he was nominated for Governor of New York. His triumphant election by an enormous majority was followed by such a fearless, progressive administration of the affairs of the state that, two years later, he seemed to his party leaders the logical man to receive the nomination for President of the United States. This judgment was vindicated by his election and his manly, straightforward service of four years at Washington. Although nominated again in 1888, he was defeated. In 1892, however, he was nominated a third time and chosen for a second term.

The least that can be said of his eight years as President is that they fulfilled the prophecies made by those who had watched his public life in less conspicuous offices.

His services to the country did not end with the close of his second term. For ten years he lived at Princeton, New Jersey, where he speedily won his place as an unofficial member of the University, the friend of the professors, the counselor of the students, the helper and inspirer of all who came in touch with him. Before he died, in 1911, he had touched the lives of thousands of young men who had gone out to take their places in the fight for true living.

XIV

An Unconquered Optimist

George Wilson's Twenty Years of Service

"HE was a splendid jewel in a shattered casket," an intimate friend said of George Wilson, a noted Scotsman who lived during the first half of the nineteenth century. "Half his life was spent in sickness or positive torture," another friend wrote. "He was constantly being blistered or cauterized or mutilated by the knife. Yet, crippled as he was by the amputation of a foot, racked with rheumatism and enfeebled by repeated hemorrhages, living, too, 'in a houseful of invalids with the shadow of the grave always hanging over it,' he preserved an unconquerable gaiety of heart, and crowded into his brief life an astonishing amount of work as a student, teacher and writer. It was written of him that he always worked as though his days were numbered, and he left on record the noble saying, 'to none is life so sweet as to those who have lost all fear to die.'"

George Wilson was born in Edinburgh, February 21, 1818, in a home where there had been much sorrow by reason of frequent bereavements. His mother watched over him tenderly. One of his first memories was of the evening visits paid by her to the bed in which he slept with his twin brother. As she bent over the boys, she would whisper the prayer of Jacob, " The God which fed me all my life long, until this day, the angel that redeemed me from all evil, bless the lads! " George was fascinated by the words, which he heard one night when the mother thought he was asleep. After that, he used to lie awake, pretending to be asleep, that he might hear the earnest prayer. The thought of the petition so often repeated was a benediction to him throughout his life.

About as soon as he could read, George began to devour books with avidity. His nurse said of his early years, " He was aye to be seen in a corner, wi' a book as big's himsel' "—probably, his biographer thinks, a volume of the first edition of the Encyclopædia Britannica.

At school he was noted for his studious qualities, but not less for his kindness of heart. He was always ready to go out of his way to help others. At one time his heart was touched by the sorrow of a boy who had lost the sight of an eye. Persecuted by his companions, he held himself aloof from their play. In order that the afflicted boy might not be robbed of his playtime, George used to stay after school hours and play with him. The thought that he was thus cutting short his own time for recreation in the precious hours of freedom, was not given consideration.

Those hours of freedom were heartily enjoyed. He delighted to ramble on Calton Hill, or look from Arthur's Seat, or climb the Salisbury Crags. On Saturday afternoons he would go with his twin brother or other companions to Leith, or Roslin Chapel, or Prestonpans. He thought nothing of a ten or fifteen mile walk after geological or botanical specimens. Thus he laid the foundation for the knowledge that enabled him later to build up the Industrial Museum of Scotland.

With eight or ten other boys he formed a " Juvenile Society for the Advancement of Knowledge." He was not yet eleven years old, and his companions were not much older. The society had its museum, filled with specimens, as well as a growing library and a journal which told of the investigations and discoveries of the juvenile members on the Saturday rambles. The weekly meetings were full of interest, especially when the members discussed such questions as these: " Whether the whale or the herring affords the more useful and profitable employment to mankind"; " Whether the camel is more useful to the Arab, or the reindeer to the Laplander."

A friend of the family, speaking of these days of character formation, said:

" At a very early age he (George) and his brothers were in the habit of noting down anything remarkable they observed in the heavens, or in the animal creation. I remember seeing a small book of these notanda, and very numerous and interesting were the topics discussed. One, I remember, was on some phenomena observed in the sky, with conjectures as to the cause. . . . No doubt their abilities were beyond those of most youths, but they owed the cultivation of them to their mother. She directed their young minds first to God, and their duty to him, then she steadily encouraged inquiry and investigation."

When Wilson determined to be a physician, he was apprenticed for four years in the laboratory of the Royal Infirmary. There he was thrown among profane companions; but the thought of his mother and of what she had taught him, enabled him to keep clean.

The years of training were marked by sorrows of which he said little. He seemed to think that his own trials and disappointments were not worthy of mention by the side of the sorrows of others. Again and again he interested himself in the misfortunes of charity patients in the infirmary, and did what he could to brighten their days. And when his sister was suffering from small-pox, and others kept away from her, he seemed unmindful of the danger and spent every evening with her.

His training in the infirmary was followed by further study until he was a licensed surgeon and physician. But he had become so fond of chemical research that he decided to devote his life to the subject. However, before he could make a real

beginning of his life work, he had a severe attack
of illness after which he never entirely recovered
his strength. Yet, a few months later, he began to
lecture regularly under appointment from the Royal
College of Surgeons. In spite of rheumatism he
continued his work, cheering everybody by the
smile behind which he hid the pain that could not
be described. After a season's exhausting work
with students, he went to London, hoping that the
change of scene and climate would bring relief.
Almost at once his hopes were dashed by an attack
of inflammation of the eyes. The sight of one eye
was at one time almost gone, but it was saved by
heroic measures.

Back in Edinburgh once more, he was looking
forward to a year of hard work when he was again
put on his back. Several weeks of intense pain
brought him to within three days of the time appointed for his first lecture of the winter term.
From the sofa he dictated two lectures, and with
these he went before his young men, upheld by a
determination to do his work in spite of pain and
weakness. Sometimes he was unable to complete
his lecture. For weeks he was unable to sleep long
at a time because of extreme pain. Yet he was
always cheerful and helpful, thoughtful of the
needs of others, the life of a home where others
were suffering as well as himself; and always his
work was done conscientiously and brilliantly.

How he was accustomed to make light of his

privations is indicated in a letter he wrote to Daniel Macmillan, who was himself in the midst of what proved to be a life-long struggle with disease:

"I have made a contract with a coachman who carries me up and down at stated hours, and I find all the consolation I can in lying all my length on the cushions and gazing with a majestic air on the pedestrians broiling in the sun. It's a fine thing, a coach, and I am the only chemist, except the Professor, who can afford one; and I am inclined to think mine the han[d]somer of the two. It is rather costly, however, and a project I have set (instead of myself) on foot of paying my way by offering my friends three penny or six penny rides, according to the distance, has not been so successful as I could wish. . . . One great consolation, however, still remains in thinking of the vexation the bootmakers must feel in knowing that my shoe soles will not be thinned by the depth of a wafer by all my locomotion."

Seldom did he allow himself to refer to his sufferings. Once when he broke through his reserve, it was only that he might help his friend, Daniel Macmillan:

"With all your sorrows I sympathize from my heart; I have learned to do so through my own sufferings. The same feelings which made you put your hand into your pocket to search among the crumbs there for the wanting coin for the beggar, lead me to search into my heart for some consola-

tion for you. . . . The last two years have been
fraught to me with such mournful experience, that
I would gladly exchange my condition for a peace-
ful grave. A bankrupt in health, hope and fortune,
my constitution shattered frightfully, and the almost certain prospect of being a cripple for life
before me, I can offer you as fervent and unselfish
a sympathy as ever one heart offered another. I
have lain awake, alone and in darkness, suffering
sore agony for hours, often thinking that the
slightest aggravation must make my condition un-
bearable and finding my only consolation in mur-
muring to myself the words patience, courage and
submission."

At last the doctors told him that he must lose his
foot or lose his life. He asked for a week's delay,
that he might have time to prepare for death. He
knew that he was not a Christian, even if his
friends did insist that he was as near perfect as a
man could be. During the week of waiting he
sought God and found him. In his own words to
a friend:

"When I was recently struggling in a great
fight of affliction, my soul and body racked and
anguished, my life hanging in the balance and
eternity in prospect, I prayed to God for light and
help, and my prayer was heard and answered."

Eleven years after, he spoke of the fact that he
got acquainted with God as a result of his operation. He said then that if he were to preach his

own funeral sermon, it would be from the text, " It is better to enter halt into life, than having two feet to be cast into hell, into the fire that never shall be quenched."

The young professor was able to walk on crutches and was looking forward to renewing his lectures when it was found that he was a sufferer from consumption. Yet he would not give up. After a season of rest he was again in the lecture room, meeting twenty young men in the morning, forty at noon, one hundred young women in the afternoon and two hundred more young men at another appointment. To all these young people he was always full of humor and helpfulness, causing them to forget their troubles and look on the bright side of life. As one of them said, " He always treated us as if we were his dearest friends." Most of them were artisans and self-supporting young people. They testified that they found him their most helpful and inspiring instructor.

He was now twenty-six years old. Feeling that he had not many years to live, he made up his mind to be more active than ever. Every moment was precious because he felt that any morning at breakfast the announcement might be made to his friends that his earthly life was done. He continued his lectures, elaborating them in every possible and profitable way. He made research that added to the store of human knowledge; he wrote a text book on chemistry, and many scientific papers.

With all this work, he found time to continue his personal ministry to the students and to write letters to invalids that he might bring a little sunshine into their lives. He responded to the pleas of some young men to conduct a Bible class for them. He did so, until failing health compelled him to give it up.

On his thirty-seventh birthday, when he had been "running a race with death" for sixteen years, he was appointed director of the new Scottish Industrial Museum. Many had objected to his appointment on the ground of his poor health, but he was selected for the position because it was felt that he could do more for the new institution than any man in full health. The sequel showed the wisdom of this decision. The new director lived for only four years, and those four years were years of great feebleness. Yet the work done by him for the Museum was most effective.

But his most effective work was done among the people whom he blessed by his presence.

Those who came to his lecture room were few compared to the thousands who rejoiced that they could see the patient sufferer who brought gladness and peace wherever he went. Their affection was evident when, on November 22, 1859, the word was whispered about the city that disease had finally brought to George Wilson his release from the body.

When his worn body was carried to old Calton

burying ground, the shops were closed, and multitudes bowed their heads on either side of the streets through which the hearse passed. " Never before was such a tribute of respect and love offered at the grave of any one of our citizens," was the comment of one of the leading men of the city.

Yet George Wilson, to whom this tribute was given, was only forty-one years of age when he died. He had given less than twenty years of service; but into those twenty years of feebleness and suffering he had crowded a lifetime of devotion to the welfare of others.

XV

Learning to Serve

How Daniel Coit Gilman Added to the World's Happiness

DANIEL COIT GILMAN was always so humble that he would have been the last to claim the verdict on his life given by those who knew him. At seventy-seven he wrote, " I have not made the most of my life; we only learn how to live when it comes time to go."

But from the days of his boyhood in the home at Norwich, Connecticut, where he was born July 6, 1831, it was evident that he thought more of the comfort and welfare of others than he did of his own happiness; in fact, he found his happiness in looking out for the happiness of others.

Devotion to a mother who brought out the best that was in him, to brothers and sisters who found him an ideal companion, to a father whose days were marked by unselfish ministry, and to God, of whom he was taught from his early childhood, made him what he was. To the end of his life he was proud to tell of the influence of his parents and their instructions by word and deed. "If ever I make anything in this world or another, I shall owe it to the blessed influence of home," he wrote when he was twenty-three years old.

That home at Norwich was a comfortable home, but it was not a wealthy home; the only wealth was the love of the members of the household for each other and the purpose of all to live in the spirit of the words of the father written to Daniel, when the boy was thirteen, just after financial reverses that compelled removal to New York City:

"The secret of being happy is in aiming at the happiness of others, doing good as we have opportunity."

The removal from the pleasant country town, with its attractive surroundings of forest and field and hill and streams whose every cataract was utilized to turn the wheels of some factory, called attention to the boy Daniel's ability to adapt himself to circumstances and make the best of everything, which made the man, Doctor Gilman, remarkable. In the country he had studied so diligently in the hours devoted to study that, at a time of need, he became the home tutor of brothers and sisters. He had adjusted his hours of recreation to such purpose that he early made a collection of minerals and natural curiosities, named by himself "A Schoolboy's Cabinet," which called forth favorable comment on all sides. He had so carefully planned and published "Our Paper," intended for absent

members of the family, that it seemed wise to trans-
fer the publication office when he went to New
York. At first the paper was written, not printed,
the ornamental headlines being the product of his
own artistic skill.

In the city his good work in school was continued, and he was soon able to pay his own academy
tuition and earn a little toward other expenses by
acting as pupil-assistant in charge of a roomful of
younger boys. And this at thirteen! He had time
for recreation, and he utilized it well. He had
dreaded the removal to the cooped-up city, yet soon
he found diversions in plenty, not only ball-playing
and skating and walking, but occupations which do
not suggest themselves to every boy.

He visited the public charitable institutions for
orphans, for the blind and for the deaf and dumb,
all the public buildings, the Navy Yard and the
government forts. In short, he knew more about
all the good things in the city in six months than
most boys knew who had lived there all their lives.
It gave him great pleasure to learn all he could
about something new—a new packet ship, for instance, or a new invention—and to come home and
tell about it. He was as ready then as he was in
later life to acquire and impart useful and interesting knowledge.

At seventeen he passed his examinations for admission to Yale College, and was so happy over
winning his way without conditions that he longed

to tell the good news by some more speedy means than a letter. It is significant that in his success his first thought was of his home. He wrote: " I feel almost as free as the wind. I am sure that if home had been within ten miles I should have set out for it on the full run this afternoon."

The years at college were years of conscientious work. He won and kept a good place in his classes. He was not content to take merely required work, but he dipped into courses that seemed then to be of little use, but later years showed that every one of them increased his fitness for the varied duties he was called to perform.

In large measure he supported himself by private teaching, by newspaper work, by lettering college diplomas, by doing cataloguing for the library. His biographer says:

" He never waited for something to do; the thing to be done always came to him. The question was never, what? but, which? By these various means he not only contributed to his own support, but was enabled to indulge his generous impulses in promoting the happiness of others and in giving substantial aid to the undertakings in which he was engaged. Working with all his might for the good of the cause, he was alike devoid of selfishness and of personal ambition."

He was an inmate of the home of his uncle, Professor James L. Kingsley, and he was considered fortunate to have such a home. But he had not

been there long before members of the household
realized that they were fortunate to have such a
guest. Fifty-six years later one of the cousins,
looking back on the association, said:

" You have mentioned his many activities; I can
say he never seemed hurried or worried amidst
them, but was always ready to lend a helping hand
to whatever was going on in the family, and was
just like a son and brother to us all."

His unselfish way of looking at life was shown
when, having been asked to deliver an address
before the three college literary societies, he announced as his subject, " The Claims of Yale College Upon Its Undergraduate Students." Rather
a new way for a student to look at his relation to
an institution!

During his freshman year, having noted in his
rambles the neglected children of the poor quarters
of lower New Haven, he proposed to several of his
classmates an afternoon Sunday school for these
children, where, in addition to religious instruction, attention should be paid to the moral
and physical well-being of the boys and girls.
Some sought to discourage him in his plans, but
he said:

" I believe we all understand that a good deal of
persevering work will be necessary, but if we can
add to the happiness or goodness of even a few we
shall be well paid."

Through the four years of the course the school

was continued, in the face of every obstacle, with such success that, just before Daniel's graduation, a public meeting was held to consider the perpetuation of the work by the erection of a suitable building and the ultimate gift of an adequate endowment. One of the city pastors spoke heartily in praise of the work of the handful of students for those whom he called savages as great as any to be found even in Kurdistan. During his talk he exclaimed:

" It is a shame to New Haven that a few young men at college in addition to their time and labor should be obliged to pay the expenses of such a school, especially that, for want of a room in which to meet, they should be compelled to hire a store at a rent of three dollars a Sunday, with the liability to be ejected at any time when the owner can secure a regular tenant."

The young student's religion was not kept for Sunday; it was a practical religion for everyday use, concerning which he was not ashamed, on occasion, to write and speak to his friends. To one of these friends he wrote, in response to a letter in which something had been said of the Christian life:

" I don't wish merely to thank you in a general way for writing as you did an expression of your sympathy, but more especially to respond to the sentiments on Christian acquaintance which you there bring out. I agree with them most fully and only regret that I did not know at an earlier time upon our journey what were your feelings upon a few such topics. I tell you, Brace, that I hate cant and all that sort of thing as much as you or anyone else can do. It is not with everyone that I could enjoy a talk upon religious subjects. I hardly ever wrote a letter on them to those whom I know best. But when anyone believes in an inner life of faith and joy and is willing to talk about it in an earnest, everyday style and tone, I do enjoy it most exceedingly. Some day or other we will have a talk upon such matters, and see how we shall agree. For one, I don't believe that all the almsgiving, useful as it is, is going to do one half as much toward reforming the world as . . . the giving of kind thoughts and acts and words to those who are in need or trouble—in short, the giving of one's self."

At the close of his college course young Gilman spent two years in Europe, his expenses being paid in large part by newspaper correspondence and other work. During this period he was an attaché of the legation at St. Petersburg. He studied in Berlin and he served as commissioner from Connecticut to the Paris Exposition of 1855.

During his absence he made an address in Manchester on American public school education that gratified those who asked him to give his help and proved of assistance in clearing up difficulties in England's educational problems.

The period of absence from home was a time of

self-examination and testing. When he reached home, he hoped to be able to decide on his life work. Should he enter the ministry? He felt much drawn to work in the pulpit, but he finally decided that his life work was to be in the educational field. As a Christian educator he felt he could be useful to his generation. He went into his chosen work with a determination to do his very best for his fellow-men.

He made his beginning at New Haven, where he was for a time assistant librarian at Yale College. After several years he succeeded the librarian. Not content to perform the slight duties believed by others to belong to his post, he magnified his office, and succeeded in bringing the library to as high a state of efficiency as circumstances permitted. He chafed under the limitations put upon him by those who felt that a college library did not call for the best efforts of the best men. He was disturbed when he was unable to secure heat for the library building which, for half the year, was either so cold it could not be used with comfort or so damp that the books molded on the shelves. Finally he resigned his office. His unselfishness was shown when he continued his efforts for better conditions, and no one was happier than he when the reforms for which he had pleaded in vain were made for his successor.

Appetite for hard work had been unabated during these years in the library. Long he served as visiting supervisor of the public schools of New Haven, again magnifying his office until, when he retired, it was necessary to employ a superintendent of city schools to take his place.

The release from the library was the signal for the real beginning of his life work. He soon became an educator of national reputation. As professor, then as secretary of the governing board, of the Sheffield Scientific School, he had much to do with the splendid development of the institution. Both the state and the national governments called him to executive educational tasks. The Universities of Wisconsin and of California called him to the presidency; the latter call, at first declined, was finally accepted. From the University of California, where his brief three years of service in the struggling young institution left a mark that endures, he was invited to undertake the molding of the new Johns Hopkins University of Baltimore. How he succeeded in making the institution the first real university of America, and how his plans influenced other universities, is a matter of history. For twenty-five years he remained at the head of this institution. Calls were made for his services by the Massachusetts Institute of Technology and by Greater New York, which desired him as the head of its public-school system. He was talked of as president of Yale University. But he remained at his work in Baltimore until the founding of the Carnegie Institution in 1902 again gave him an opportunity to mold a giant foundation in a wise and enduring manner.

The twenty-five years in Baltimore were characterized by the same hunger for hard work for which he had always been known. He was the first head of the Johns Hopkins hospital. He worked for the freedmen, he was a Civil Service reformer, he was active in the American Bible Society's councils, he helped to frame Baltimore's new charter, he outlined the plan of the Russell Sage Foundation, and he was a member of the Peabody Education Board. At the request of President Cleveland he served on the commission sent to settle the dispute between Venezuela and British Guiana. His associates declared that the satisfactory conclusion of the commission's work was largely due to his knowledge and his wise suggestions. His familiarity with surveying, which was acquired when he took one of the optional courses at Yale for which some of his friends could at the time see no use, contributed much to the success of this work.

So the time was passed until, in 1906, he sent a photograph to a favorite sister, on which he wrote the legend, "Facing seventy-five!"

She answered:

"Yes, but facing it with courage, hope and good cheer! Not idly looking back on unfinished work, not bemoaning what might have been, but standing firm in the present, resolutely looking forward, assured that

> " 'The best is yet to be—
> The last of life for which the first was planned.' "

Two years later, on October 13, 1908, Daniel Coit Gilman was suddenly called home to the land of which he had written some years before, quoting the last words of General Armstrong:

" How will the next world seem? Perfectly fair and natural, no doubt. We ought not to fear death. It is friendly."

Bibliography

For the convenience of those who wish to read more fully about the men who figure in the chapters of Men Who Conquered, a list of the biographies consulted or quoted by the author is given.

BANCROFT, GEORGE: "Life and Letters of George Bancroft," by M. A. DeWolfe Howe; Charles Scribner's Sons.

CHILDS, GEORGE W.: "Recollections"; J. B. Lippincott Co.

CLEVELAND, GROVER: "Grover Cleveland," in Lives of the Presidents Series, by W. O. Stoddard; Frederick A. Stokes Co.

DANA, RICHARD HENRY: "Richard Henry Dana," by Charles Francis Adams; Houghton, Mifflin and Co.

DODGE, WILLIAM E.: "William E. Dodge, the Christian Merchant," by C. Martyn; Funk and Wagnalls Co.

EASTMAN, CHARLES A.: "An Indian Boyhood"; Doubleday, Page and Co.

GILMAN, DANIEL COIT: "Life of Daniel Coit Gilman," by F. Franklin; Dodd, Mead and Co.

HOWE, SAMUEL GRIDLEY: "Dr. Samuel Gridley Howe, Philanthropist," by F. R. Sanborn; Funk and Wagnalls Co.

MUIR, JOHN: "Story of My Boyhood and Youth"; Houghton, Mifflin Co.

PEARSONS, DANIEL K.: "Life of Dr. D. K. Pearsons," by E. Williams; The Pilgrim Press.

PITMAN, ISAAC: "Life of Sir Isaac Pitman," by A. Baker Pitman.

RIIS, JACOB: "The Making of an American," and "The Old Town," by Jacob Riis; The Macmillan Co.

SIMS, J. MARION : "Story of My Life"; D. Appleton and Co.

WESTINGHOUSE, GEORGE : "George Westinghouse, His Life and Achievements," by Francis A. Leupp; Little, Brown and Co.

WILSON, GEORGE : "Memoirs of George Wilson," by his sister; Edinburgh, 1860 (out of print).